The S

The Story Chair

Memories from the Past

Stories from the personal histories of the Hillis, Switzer, Belfry, Sherman, and Ney clans

Compiled by
Margaret Belfry Lynn

Shoreline

Cover design and graphics: Sarah Robinson
Photographs from the author's collection

Shoreline
23 Ste-Anne, Ste-Anne-de-Bellevue , QC H9X 1L1
shoreline@sympatico.ca www.shorelinepress.ca
514.457.5733

Printed in Canada by Marquis Imprimeur

ISBN 978 1- 896754-59-8

Dépôt légal: Library and Archives Canada
and Bibliothèque nationale de Quebec

To our parents,
Mary Hillis and **Norman Belfry,**
who lovingly shared the stories of our ancestors,
and
to our children and grandchildren,
who will add their own colours to the family tapestry.

Acknowledgements

To cousins who have recounted tales of loved ones, thereby refreshing our memories, and to new friends across the globe who have generously shared their knowledge, expertise and enthusiasm, we offer heartfelt thanks. By their very nature, stories tend to vary in the telling so my apologies for any inaccuracies which have resulted.

Our mother Mary's foresight in chronicling the last 75 years of her life and the lives of those who were part of it has offered a treasure trove of insight, wisdom and information. Without her diaries and scrapbooks this project could never have been realized.

Membership in the Quebec Family Historical Society was pivotal in beginning this search. Their seminars and workshops give encouragement to neophyte genealogists and their library and media collections are valuable resources. Libraries in Hanover and Bradford, Ontario; Archives Collections in Montreal, Quebec City and Toronto, both on location and on line; and historical newspaper articles from *The Hanover Post* added to our store of information. The awesome collections of the Family History Library of the Latter Day Saints in Salt Lake City, Utah, further added to our awareness of past history and supplied important lost data, as has the Irish Palatinate Association in Limerick, Ireland, whose colourful journals about our German connection offered interesting glimpses of the past. Sincere and grateful thanks must also be reserved for the generous help and friendship given to us in Assenheim, Germany. Our welcome there as long-lost family members will remain a highlight of this search for our roots.

I am deeply grateful to Judith Isherwood and Shoreline Press for their positive encouragement in this process and their willingness to publish my material.

Special appreciation is reserved for the participation of my brother, Ronald Keith Belfry, whose memories and affection have been a joyful part of my life. And to my husband, William (Bill) Benedict Lynn, my rock and confidant, who has pulled me through the complexities of 'computer ease' with gentle good humour, and who has been my caring supporter in this venture as in the adventures of our delightful yesterdays, our busy todays, and for the rest of our tomorrows, I offer my undying thanks and love.

Margaret Belfry Lynn,
2007

Contents

Layer by Layer

Monet, the master craftsman, embellished his canvases with amazing colours. First one pigment was applied, then another, each careful addition adding to the vibrancy of his creation.

Is this, I wonder, how our own personal canvases have been fashioned? Has our uniqueness unfolded *layer by layer* in part because of the vision and energy of the myriad forefathers who people our past? What a fascinating concept.

Monet's creations became world-renowned wonders. We, however, are *works in progress,* absorbing aspects of the past and daily building dimension and texture. Carefully we harvest each threadbare clue, hoard details about those people from whom we've sprung and wonder where and how they became part of our story. Family sagas and buried memories, too, add variegated hues to our layering.

The voices of our ancestors and their lives as enthusiastic pioneers and visionaries have helped to define us as family. Our nation is inhabited by countless other families such as these.

Hopefully these recounted memories and documented items will contribute another layer for the children of tomorrow, our heirs. Read them, savour them, and appreciate our small part in the grand plan of human history.

The Story Chair

It sits serenely in my sunroom in a puddle of golden sunlight, basking in the memories of past lives and family lore. But on those 'long-ago-nights' by the fire when it was newly crafted, it provided a focal point around which to snuggle while listening to exciting tales -- of flights from Germany in search of religious freedom, of frightening sea voyages, of our grandparents' treks through the woods to new homesteads.

Now it conjures up a vision of how life was 'back then'. This chair has traveled far from that small Switzer cabin in southern Ontario where it was crafted.

Its first move from the Switzer home was to the Hillis homestead some miles over the hills and down the road. Then, following new owners, it travelled to several Ontario towns and even to cities. But wherever it settled, it was treasured. Its last role, before retiring to my sunroom, was as a 'Story Chair' in my Westmount, Quebec, classroom. What power it held there! The minute I sat in it, my ten-year-old Selwyn House boys dropped whatever task was at hand, grabbed a cushion and eagerly awaited the magic of another time and another place.

The Chair made by Benjamin Switzer
Circa 1850

Each year the boys were told its story and that it was my very special possession. One day a couple of them became a little too physical while awaiting the arrival of their French teacher. One unfortunate young man was unceremoniously flipped over the back, and some of the rungs became unhinged. Horrors! Faces were long and very serious when I returned to the class several periods later. In fact, I thought something dreadful must have happened.

Finally a tentative hand inched up and explanations tumbled out. I was quickly assured that Monsieur Rondeau, their French teacher, whom I knew to be a wonderful craftsman, had already carefully glued the rungs back in place, and that they were very, very sorry. I was touched that they had grasped its uniqueness and its importance to me.

No, I didn't have the heart to chastise them. Their discomfort was evident. Later, the restorers handled it quite reverently, acknowledging that it was indeed a treasure from the past. I was assured that the one who would work on it had learned the trade at his father's knee, and would treat it with the respect it richly deserved. And he did. How pleased Benjamin Switzer, my Great-Great-Grandfather would have been to know that his work was still so valued.

It is not a fancy chair. Its rough shape had been fashioned by Great-Great-Grandfather Switzer's hand in the mid 1850's, and then painted with lamp-black. The naively stenciled designs on the headrest reflect the handwork of an unsigned, untrained artist. Worn rockers attest to the fact that many feet have slid along them over the years. It is small and low, but was just perfect for story time for his wife, my petite Great-Grandma Switzer (the former Mary Leonard), her many children clustered expectantly at her feet by the fire.

And it is still very much treasured by me.

It speaks to me of our ancestors, of their struggles to carve out an existence in a harsh, unforgiving land, and of the rich heritage with which they have endowed our lives.

I, too, have heard those stories while sitting in rapt attention curled around its rockers. The exodus of our German forefathers as they were uprooted from their idyllic corner of the Pfalz region, and subsequently created new lives and homes in Ireland was fascinating. How must that have felt?

A favorite saga was about the birth of a great-great-great-grandfather on the rolling ocean waves, leading eventually to the rough reality of life in a frigid log cabin. We find it hard to comprehend this when considering our own creature comforts. And going to school barefoot, hearing about the excitement of the first sounds from a crackly crystal set? These visions seem as far from our reality as those fairy tales of old.

I can almost hear the warm, vibrant voice of our mother, Mary Hillis Belfry, great-granddaughter of that story-telling Grandma Switzer, as she recounted those happenings to us, along with frequent dollops of Grimm's tales, lilting Irish lullabies or recitations learned for school presentations.

Our Stories

Let me share some of those stories, starting with Mary's growing-up years. Mary left many diaries, scrapbooks full of newspaper clippings about people whom she knew and cared for, notebooks of poetry written in the blush of first love, and so many wonderful anecdotes. Our lives were peppered with stories of growing up in a world quite different from the one with which we were familiar.

Let's follow the paths she took while growing up, going to school and meeting the love of her life. Later we will meet some of the fascinating family members who peopled her world. During our journey we will be introduced to several large families whose colourful ancestors came to Canada via different routes. This exodus has been reenacted with increasing frequency over the ensuing years across our land. Many, many homesteaders came: eager youths, skilled and unskilled men looking for work, young women who hoped for more opportunities, and whole families looking for a new home and better lives for their children. They journeyed from the far corners for religious and political freedom, for survival, or for the sheer joy of seeing new places. With them came their customs, their wisdom, their joys and their sorrows.

Freedom, fulfillment and adventure were what many of them found.
Their story is ours. Let's settle down around the Story Chair and listen while Mary's memories and stories record the happenings of her loved ones for posterity.

Mary Hillis, 1907 - 2000

Little Mary

Little Mary perched silently on the edge of the rocking chair beside the huge wood stove. She was transfixed. The worn black runners were now quiet after the anxious rocking of the morning. And, as well, the little girl remained still, still, still.

The rest of the steamy farm kitchen was awash in activity. Huge pots of water had been simmering on the stove, their billowing vapor turning the summer morning into a moist sauna. And Grandma Switzer and Aunt Mary were busy, busy with warm towels and quick steps to and from her parent's big front bedroom.

Mary remained quiet, watching. Big sister, Florence, was out in the meadow bringing the cows in from pasture, sister Beatrice was happily playing tag with the chickens, but little Mary could not drag herself away. She just knew that this was going to be a very special day.

Then Mary heard it. It sounded like the baby kittens that she'd seen in the barn, the ones that were bathed in water and then disappeared. Were there to be more kittens, she wondered? Maybe the pots of water were for them....

All of a sudden, her Grandma Switzer danced into the kitchen holding a tiny little bundle. There, wrapped in a blanket, was a wrinkled, wee baby, all red and squirmy, cradled lovingly in her strong arms.

Grandma said, "Look Mary. Come and see your new baby sister. She is going to be named Jennie Benetta."

How excited Mary felt! It was even better than the new dolly that she'd been hoping for. What fun to have a real baby to watch over and another little sister for a playmate.

Her sisters would be so excited when they found out what had happened!

But then she paused. A very sobering thought popped into her head. She remembered that the kittens had not been alive after their bath. Then she looked at the water on the stove.

As Grandma left the room, Mary quietly slipped off the chair and grasped the dipper hanging by the sink. She went to the stove, dipped water from a pot, then dumped it into the sink. Again and again -- carefully, oh so carefully -- she did this. Working quickly, she had almost completed her task when Grandma came back into the kitchen. Mary tried to hide the dipper, but alas, Grandma spotted it.

"Mary, what on earth are you doing with that dipper?" she gasped.

Mary started to cry. She cried so hard that she could barely be understood. Finally the words tumbled out between sobs. She didn't want her new baby sister to suffer the destiny that had befallen the stray kittens.

Grandma quickly wrapped her strong arms around Mary, assuring her that that was not going to happen, and together they went into the bedroom. There her mother lay smiling, and her tiny new baby sister was snuggled there, too. Together they were curled into a cuddly warm ball in the big, plump bed.

Mary was entranced. "Oh, yes," she thought, "This really *is* a very special day."

How right she was. It was so special that she and Jennie, later to be called Jean, formed an unshakeable bond, which they both treasured for the rest of their lives.

That was 9 June 1912, the day that the fourth daughter was born to our grandfather, Wilson Thomas Hillis, and his beloved wife, Margaret Lavina Switzer Hillis. With them lived their other children: Florence Amelia, born 10 December 1904;

our mother, Mary Marguerite, born 27 February 1907; and Beatrice Luella, born 14 March 14 1909.

The Hillis family, who lived comfortably in the rolling farmlands of Ontario, was now complete.

Mary, Florence, Jennie (Jean) and Beatrice Hillis
Summer, 1912

So far this small family had remained relatively untouched by news events of the world at large. Reports of the shocking sinking of the *unsinkable* Titanic had likely not touched them. Ziegfeld's Follies, a great success in New York, was of little interest, and it is doubtful that they were aware the world would soon be shaken by the horrors of a World War.

They were just a small, typical farm family, busily creating a home and identity in the rich farmlands near Hanover, Ontario, where the Rocky Saugeen River still flows gently nearby.

But what twist of fate placed this young family in this particular spot near Hanover in Southern Ontario?

Hillis family

Horse and buggy

Jennie and Mary

Dad with daughters

Margaret and
Wilson Hillis

winter fun

Mom Hillis

Sisters

The Hillis Family

Hillis Genealogical Data

First known Hillis forefather:
James (Our Great-Great-Grandfather): b.1799 **-** d**.**1898 County Monaghan, Ireland.
m. **Matilda** b.?? - d.1877, Details unknown

Second generation:
Samuel: b.1835 Ireland, to U. S., dates unknown. Children: **Albert:** doctor in Berthold, North Dakota, and **George:** b. 16 Dec. 1893, Crystal, North Dakota,
James William (Our Great-Grandfather): b.1837 Ireland - d. Jan. 1900, Ontario
1) m. **Mary Duke:** b. ?? - d. 8 June 1877, d/o James Duke, Mono Mills, in Caledon, Ont., Co. of Peel, m. 1859
2) m. **Mary Sinclair**: b. 31 July 1852 - d. June 1920, m. 20 March 1878

Third Generation
Children of first marriage of James Hillis to Mary Duke:
Jennie Ann: b.1863 - d. Dec. 1892 in Island Lane, North Dakota, no children. m. John McIntyre 1892
John James: b.1866 - d. Sept. 1941, m. Mary E Purvis: b.1866 - d.13 Oct. 1978
Mary Elizabeth: b.1870 - d. May 1913 in Toronto, Ont., single, no children
Wilson Thomas (Our Grandfather): b. 7 April 1877, - d. 22 Dec. 1955, in Hanover, Ont.
1) m. Margaret Lavina Switzer, b. 4 Nov. 1877 - d. 18 Mar. 1930, Hanover, Ont.
2) m. Two other marriages as helpers on farm: 1) Florence Henry, Brampton, 2) Jessie Marshall

Children of second marriage of James Hillis to Mary Sinclair:
Samuel Joseph Alexander: b 7 Oct. ?? - d. 1980 in Florida, USA.
Ella Matilda: b. 13 August 1884 - d. July 1972, wife of Wesley Grant, Toronto, Ont.

Fourth generation

Children of Wilson Hillis and Margaret Switzer:

Florence Amelia: b. 10 Dec. 1904 - d. Normanby, - d. 6 Dec. 1994, m. 14 July 1922 to **James Emerson Hudson**, Hanover, Ont.

Mary Marguerite (Our Mother): b. 27 Feb. 1907, Normanby Twp - d. 25 Sept. 2000, Walkerton, Ont.

m. 13 Nov. 1928, to **Norman Ambrose Belfry:** b. 21 Sept 1899, Victoria Harbor - d. 8 July 1974, London, Ont.

Beatrice Luella: b. 14 March 1909, Normanby Twp - d. 28 Sept 1982, Mildmay, Ont.

m. 14 June 1928 **Oliver George Harrison:** b. 1903 - d. 1979, Mildmay, Ont.

Jean (Jennie Benetta): b. 9 June 1912 - d. 27 Aug. 1995, Hanover, Ont.

m. 4 June 1938 to **Charles Muir Fursman:** b. Normanby, Twp, 7 July 1901 - d. 1 Dec 1982, Toronto, Ont.

Children of the Fifth and Sixth generations

Florence and Emerson Hudson had:

John Wilson (Jack): m. **Katherine Scott Pentland** 11 Sept. 1945 in Scotland.

Three children **Karen**, **Lynda** and **Janet**

James Emerson (Jim): m. **Mary Isabel Stewart** 15 Nov. 1947.

Four children: **Marion**, **James**, **Carole** and **John**,

Gary Wayne: m. **Dianne Gateman** 28 July 1967, Hanover.

Two children: **Randy** and **Rodney**.

Mary and Norman Belfry had

Ronald Keith: m. **Margaret Lillian Reilly** 21 April 1956, Waterloo, (b. 28 Nov. 1933 - d. 29 Jan. 2007 in Portugal while on holiday).

Three children: **Colleen**, **Joanne** and **Wanda**.

Margaret Esther (**Recorder of these stories**): m. **William Benedict (Bill) Lynn** on 17 Dec. 1960, France

Two children: **Heather-Anne** and **Brian Alexander**

Beatrice and Oliver Harrison had:

Earl: m. **Joan Wilkenson**, 1950, Teaswater.
Four Children: **Bette Ann**, **Mary Jane**, **Robert**, **John**

Jean: m. **Harvey "Jiggs" Liesemer,** 1958 Mildmay
Three children: **Daniel, Peter** and **David**

Ross: m. **Ann Goetz,** 1956 Kitchener.
Six children: **Richard**, **Colleen, Alan**, **Kim**, **Ross**, and **Nadine**.

Alan: m. **Rolande,** 1963, Thunder Bay
Two children: **Earl** and **Jean**

Jean and Charles Fursman, had no children.

Our branch of the Hillis family came from Ireland, quite likely from either County Monaghan or Dublin. Records suggest that our first known forefather, James Hillis, was born in Monaghan in 1799 and died in 1898. There were a number of Hillis families in the Monaghan area but we have not been able to discover all the pertinent details of James's family. As more and more of the Irish records become Internet accessible, we hope more specifics will emerge. It is an interesting phenomenon that many of our generation only now want to know the details of their families.

How sad that we didn't have the foresight to ask these questions when the folks who had the answers were still alive.

Our particular part of the Hillis story really begins when this first James's two sons, eleven-year-old James William, our great-grandfather (b.1837), and thirteen-year-old Samuel (b.1835), came to Canada from Dublin.

This was in 1848 when the potato famine was at its height, and there is little doubt that this dreadful factor was a catalyst to their voyage. In fact, the decade between 1841 and 1851 saw over one third of the Irish population disappear either through death by starvation, or by emigration.

The potato was the primary source of food for the working class. One Internet report about Irish history tells us that "*Their acre of garden feeds them the year through, nine months on potatoes and the other three on oaten bread from their own oats.*" When we read that a labourer could eat up to fourteen pounds of potatoes a day we understand the importance of this root vegetable. The air-borne spore affecting the potato crop could and did wipe out the whole crop, whether in the soil or in storage, in a matter of days. Sufficient supplies of potatoes became nonexistent and the resultant famine was horrendous. Many families were devastated.

This situation created anger and frustration. In some areas the English landlords took the greater percent of the crops for their own use, leaving little or nothing for those who toiled in the fields. Soon those who could escape to a new life did so. The emigrating Irish sailed for North America in very poorly maintained ships beginning in 1846. Many died at sea, or contracted typhus or other diseases while in quarantine at places like Grosse Isle in the St. Lawrence near Quebec City, then carried these germs to Montreal and other locations as they moved on.

What was the occupation of James' and Samuel's father? This we do not know. We do know that their parents were called John and Abigail. Quite likely John was not a landowner, although he could have lived and worked for one, but the details of their lives remain a mystery to us.

However, it is clear that these were very difficult times for everyone, and survival was very much in doubt. One can hardly imagine how those two young boys were able to survive in a new land, let alone prosper. Did they come on their own? Were they travelling with family members or friends? Some Hillis documentation shows that a William and Mary Hillis immigrated to Canada in 1848 so it is possible they were relatives who took the boys under their care. According to Ontario archival records, a William and Mary Hillis and their eight children became homesteaders in Bentinck Township.

This was not far from where James and Samuel began their own farms later. It would seem then that they possibly journeyed together.

Certainly prospects of a healthy life in Ireland were very slim indeed. We wonder if their departure for Canada was the unselfish gesture of desperate parents trying to secure a better life for their sons. After arrival in Canada, the brothers lived with an aunt in Caledon, County of Peel, Ontario, until setting out on their own, so it is likely this was their planned destination.

This part of Canada was largely uncharted, and must have been quite overwhelming. Ingenuity, tenacity and sheer bravado would have been valuable assets for survival in this environment.

Gradually more sections of the country were becoming open to homesteaders so when James was 24, he and Sam headed north to seek their fortune as farmers in the Hanover area. Their roots were firmly planted here - as this is where James was to live for the rest of his life. They chose Lots 7 and 8, Concession 18, and here they built a rude shanty, their first Canadian home.

After a few years Sam took the south half of these lots and James took the north. Each farm was about four miles from the town of Hanover, Ontario, and consisted of 100 acres of the finest clay loam.

Much later Sam would leave Ontario and go to the United States where he would remain to start his own family.

First began the daunting task of chopping down enough trees for space, and for logs needed for a permanent dwelling. Eventually many trees were cleared from the dense bush but James left acres of good forest for the needs of future generations.

After his log cabin was completed, James's thoughts turned to a young woman whom he'd fancied in Caledon. In 1859 he returned there to marry Miss Mary Duke, daughter of Thomas and June, who was to become our great-grandmother. James and Mary were married in Mona Mills, Ontario, by Rev. John W. Savage. Their children, Jane Ann (Jennie), John-James, Mary Elizabeth, and Wilson Thomas gave them great pleasure but soon their lives as a family were seriously threatened.

Sadly, on 8 June 1877 Mary died at the age of 38 when Wilson was only three months old. How difficult it must have been for a widowed farmer to raise young children without the benefits of the social services we now take for granted.

We do know that neighbours and family members came to the rescue in these circumstances, often taking charge of each other's children in their own homes when the need arose. Folks helped each other with barn-raising, harvesting and many other farm chores, whether they were relatives or not. One can imagine that the line between family and friends must have almost evaporated in many cases. This created a marvelous sense of community, thus strengthening our land.

After Mary's death James was a lonely man and sorely missed the companionship of a partner and a mother for his children. The year after he was widowed the 41-year-old-father returned to Caledon and married Mary Sinclair (born in Caledon, Ontario, 31 July, 1852), daughter of Alex and Jane Sinclair. Their wedding took place on 20 March 1878. Theirs was a long and blessed marriage. They joyfully welcomed two children, Samuel and Ella Matilda.

Now the Hillis family portrait was complete. Together James and Mary and their family of six children enjoyed happiness and forged an enviable reputation in the community.

The Hillis Homestead: the Hillis family and their new home, circa 1880s

By 1882 this farm had grown and prospered, however that first small homestead was unfortunately destroyed by fire. Soon an impressive, eleven-roomed, white brick home was erected on the site. Construction was by James Lock of Walkerton, Ontario.

In 1884 the farm was further enhanced by the addition of an impressive 54' by 80' barn. It was an elegant property and a homestead of which to be proud. A driving shed and sheep pen were added to the barn as the need became evident. These were the buildings that our mother, Mary, and her sisters later shared, and they remain today as a testament to the drive and industry of their forefathers.

James Hillis and Family
Back Row: Mary Elizabeth, Wilson Thomas, Jane Ann (Jennie) (McIntyre), and John James
Front Row: Ella Matilda (Grant), James, Mary Sinclair Hillis, Samuel James. Circa *1890s*

Jennie Ann, who became Mrs. John McIntyre, died at Island Lane, North Dakota, in December 1892 at the age of 29 years. As we can see in this photo, her likeness had been added later. No doubt this is because she lived in the western United States and was not able to be there for the group photo. It is significant that her "spot" was carefully left so that a suitable photo could be included later.

In thinking about how and why she was living there I began to wonder if she went west at the urging of her Uncle Samuel who had headed west some years earlier. Certainly young single women were not in great supply in the west at that time so this writer is supposing that she was invited out to visit and possibly make a suitable marriage.

Mary Elizabeth, who never married, died in Toronto in May 1913 of double pneumonia. She was our mother, Mary's, namesake.

Wilson Thomas, our grandfather, married **Margaret Lavina Switzer**, 12 Dec. 1900, and died at age 79 on 22 Dec. 1955 following a stroke. Their story is included in this document and is an interesting part of our history.

John James was married 24 Dec. 1890 at Bentinck to **Mary E. Purvis** (b 1866 - d 1936), daughter of George Purvis and Emma Pringle. (Mary Purvis was lovingly referred to as Aunt Polly and John James was *always* called Uncle John James). They made their home in Hanover in later years. After Aunt Polly's death he enjoyed frequent lengthy visits to the homestead, where brother Wilson and his family lived.

James's daughter from his second marriage was **Ella Matilda** who became Mrs. Wesley Grant, Her husband, **Wesley Grant,** was in the printing business. They and their daughter Mary (later Landerkin) lived in Toronto, Ontario. Mary Hillis, our mother, shared their home while attending Toronto Normal School.

Ella and Sam with their parents

Son **Samuel** became a doctor, went to the States and married **Katinka Otterson**. They lived in Minneapolis for many years before retiring to Florida. And what an interesting story that was! Recently I heard about how and why he went to the United States and it is the stuff of novels, as we will discover.

Sam's Story

Uncle Sam and Aunt Tinka visited in Hanover a number of times, either by themselves or sometimes with their children. Mary and their daughter Dikka became friends in later years, and kept up the yearly exchange of cards and family information that had begun with Katinka and Sam.

As a child I remember how delighted we all were when the card bearing their names and often family photos arrived in the mail. What an attractive family they were. Their Nordic good looks through Katinka's Scandinavian heritage seemed far more glamorous than the folks that we knew. On Mary's death I, too, have shared family news so the tradition of keeping in touch continues. Recently, in thinking about this family record I asked Dikka, who lives in Gig Harbour, Washington, to tell me something about her parents. Their story proves that fate has a very mischievous way of directing our futures and fortunes.

Sam graduated from Walkerton, Ontario, High School and then from Trinity Medical College (University Of Toronto) in 1904. A cousin, Dr. Albert Hillis, who, we believe was the son of the first Samuel who had earlier gone to the States, was the first medical practitioner in Berthold, North Dakota. These Hillis folks had been keeping in touch, so our assumption that they were part of the first Sam's family was accurate. Albert asked Samuel to take over his medical practice for a month in order that he and his bride (Lorraine Walther) could honeymoon in Tacoma, Washington.

It turned out that the honeymooners quite liked Tacoma and decided to make their permanent home there. Indeed, they stayed in Tacoma for the rest of their lives.

Because Walther was a name I had not heard before, I searched the Internet for information about Lorraine's family and about this western community. I learned that her father, Frederich C. Walther, was one of the first settlers in the community of Berthold and was the builder-owner of the first store. Later a school, railroad, parks, and cemetery were added with his help. So many settlements and communities that sprouted all over North America had adventurous people like Lorraine's father to thank for such vision and industry.

Berthold was a small community near Minot in North Dakota that began to develop around 1900. At Albert's urging, Samuel stayed in Berthold as the town's second doctor. He was elected the town's first mayor and remained there until 1935.

Around 1909 Samuel married Sara Darton from Stoughton, Wisconsin, a sister of Sam's friend who was a storeowner in Berthold. One can imagine that these communities were small, and as settlers moved west, young women were very much sought after as brides. Having an available sister or a cousin would be quite an asset to the development of the area. Quite possibly this is how Jennie Ann, Samuel's older step-sister, came to be married and living in North Dakota, where she died as a young woman.

Sam and Sara honeymooned with Mr. and Mrs. Herman Sampson in Rio, Wisconsin. Hotels were likely not very much in evidence as yet so people stayed with friends when they travelled away from home. Most communities were fairly isolated and folks were delighted to have company. While there the honeymooners were entertained at dinner in the home of a Lutheran Minister, Otto Christian Ottersen. At that time their daughter, Katinka, who also shared in entertaining the guests, was around nine years old.

A few years later, when Katinka was only 16 years old, her father died. From there she went to live with her aunt in Berthold, and while in Berthold she completed her high school studies.

The First World War was ravaging Europe at the time and Sam was part of it, serving as a doctor in France. While he was away Katinka and Samuel's wife, Sara, became fast friends.

Upon completion of high school Katinka went to the Twin Cities (Minneapolis and St. Paul), graduated from Business College and became secretary to the manager of the Cunard Star Lines.

When Sam returned safely from France, he and Sara began to plan a home in Berthold. These settlements had little in the way of shops, so Sara visited the Twin Cities to buy the furnishings, linens, china and silver for the home Sam was building for them. While there she stayed with her young friend Katinka who was delighted to help her friend Sara make suitable choices.

Unfortunately, shortly after the home was completed, Sara died.

Samuel continued his contact with the Army Medical Corps after the war, and on one occasion he was on a two-week training session in Fort Snelling near the Twin Cities. A relative suggested that he contact Katinka whom Samuel had heard about but did not remember meeting.

He did call on her and they went to Minnehaha Falls for their first afternoon outing. They both must have enjoyed that afternoon 'date' very much, because they soon began keeping in touch via notes and letters, phone calls, and then visits back and forth.

Eventually it became obvious that a romance was in the wind. Everyone's eyebrows rose! Katinka was 20 years younger than Samuel - and a Lutheran! Samuel must have been quite smitten so decided to explore the Lutheran beliefs. Following these studies he was confirmed in the Lutheran faith by a pastor in Minot, and he and Katinka made wedding plans.

On October 24th, 1923 Samuel and Katinka were married. In later years they lived in St. Paul, Minnesota, where Sam's practice flourished. Florida beckoned, so following his retirement they moved to Bradenton in the Sunshine State where they spent the rest of their lives. What a wonderful story.

They were stunning, tall, fair-haired, and quite exotic looking to our unsophisticated eyes. Perhaps it was the Nordic characteristics that Katinka brought to the family. I well remember their visits to the homestead where Aunt 'Tinka' awed us by wearing silky lounging pajamas, not the usual farm attire in the mid-1940s.

Our father, Norman Belfry, and Katinka Hillis, circa 1947

Sam and Katinka were affectionate, friendly, and everyone flocked around to meet them and bask in their aura. My brother, Ron, and I had a good laugh every time we heard 'Little Mary', our mother, tell about the time as a child she had sent a Christmas card addressed to her uncle, with the only address being **'Uncle Sam, U.S.A.'**. Sophistication had not been part of this little girl's life on the farm.

And what happened to Sam's namesake, the brother who came to Canada with James and then headed to the States? While details are rather sketchy, I also remember Christmas letters from the Newlove family who lived in Washington, D.C. It is only recently that I began to connect this family with that first Samuel. Those annual greetings came from Vangie (Evangeline) Newlove, who I believe was the first Sam's descendent. At her death her daughter Ivadel continued the letters. When we and our teenaged children were travelling through Washington one hot summer day some decades ago, we thought it would be interesting to meet her, so contacted Ivadel and invited her to be our guest for a picnic. She readily agreed but insisted that she prepare the picnic. When we called to pick her up we discovered that her delightful picnic was daintily spread on her dining room table and she was a charming hostess.

For the rest of our day together she played tour guide *par excellence* as she directed us to fascinating sites in her city.

She had graduated from George Washington University in 1921, with extra studies in teaching children with special needs. In her career as an inner city teacher she had faced many educational challenges. Eagerly she shared her city with us.

The amazing Washington Cathedral, her work area, and of course the parks and political delights of that great city were explained in fascinating detail. Her insight made the experience so much more memorable. How we wished that we lived closer and could have continued the friendship that blossomed so brightly that day.

There were often surprises as the layers were peeled in this search for clues about members of our clan. And this happened here as I started to read one of Mary's mid- eighties diaries. She was accustomed to tucking clippings, sayings, poems, and obituaries among the tiny pages, and this diary was full of treasures. A small clipping from the *Washington Post* of 10 May 1984 fell onto my lap as I read. My attention was caught. It was an obituary for a George H. Newlove dated 5 October 1984, which I feel sure gives some additional clues about Samuel and the Newlove families. A subsequent Google check has fleshed out further interesting details as follows:

George Hillis Newlove was born in Crystal, North Dakota, on Dec 16, 1893, son of Rev. Samuel Newlove and Vangie Hillis Newlove, a pioneer school teacher. George followed in his mother's footsteps as an educator and this led to a distinguished career as one of the nation's leading academic accountants. He received Ph.D. degrees from universities in St. Paul's Minnesota and University of Illinois, following which he was also granted a CPA designation, making him one of the first five people who had such a rare combination of Ph.D. and CPA. He became a member of the faculty at University of Texas in 1928, where he participated in teaching and developing graduate studies. Oil had been discovered on the university campus about that time and he was instrumental in helping them enlarge their facilities substantially. He was the author of many academic books and articles and supervised countless graduate students. He retired in 1967 and died in 1984.

So it would seem that Samuel had a rich life in America and his children became valuable educators. Dabbling in genealogy has interesting rewards.

Ella (Hillis) Grant, Wilson Hillis, Ivadel and Vangie (Hillis) Newlove, Wesley Grant, Jessie Marshall Hillis visiting at the home farm in Hanover

Dr Sam, Katinka and son James

Great-Grandfather Hillis died in Hanover in early 1900 at the age of 63 years as the result of a kick by a horse. According to his obituary in the *Hanover Post* of 15 March 15 1900, he was

A hardworking, wiry man who had hardly known illness until a fall from his horse affected his heart and kidneys, and from which he was unable to recover.

Great-Grandfather James Hillis

He was described in this news account as:

A man honest in his dealings, and a faithful member of the Methodist Church where he taught Sunday school, and carried out many other church responsibilities faithfully throughout his lifetime.

His widow, Mrs. Mary Hillis, lived with her daughter Ella, Mrs. Wesley Grant, in Toronto after the death of her husband.

She died on August 22nd, 1924 as the result of a paralytic stroke. *The Hanover Post* of August 28, 1924 said that she would be remembered:

Mrs. Hillis was one of those large-hearted motherly women whom it is a delight to know. The Hillis home was the scene of many jolly gatherings where genuine, wholesome hospitality radiated - occasions which are all too few now as Hanover has grown bigger and people do not know each other so well.

I imagine that that particular newspaper reporter would be quite amazed now to see how the town of Hanover has prospered with many industries, and expanded far out onto those surrounding farms.

After James Hillis died, the farm became the property of his son, Wilson Thomas, our grandfather. And this brings us to the family home, and to Mary and her sisters.

Wilson and Margaret Hillis with his sister, Ella, and her husband, Wesley Grant

Growing Up

"Little Mary" was certainly petite, but she was given the diminutive "little" so as not to be confused with her beloved namesake, Aunt Mary Hillis, her father's eldest sister, or her Aunt Mary Switzer, her mother's twin sister.

Mary described her home in her own memoir so that her future grandchildren could picture what life was like when she was growing up. Listen while she tells us about life as children in their beautiful farm home.

Mary at dress-up time

"Let me see too!" Florence, Beatrice and Mary

i. "Downstairs we had a kitchen, pantry, large dining room, a parlor, two bedrooms and a sewing room which was later made into a bathroom. We had two upstairs, one over the kitchen, which was just one big room.

ii. The room over the kitchen became our playroom, a perfect place for four girls to giggle away the cold winter days. The walls were whitewashed so we loved to use them for our artwork." What a way to decorate walls.

iii. "The front upstairs had three large bedrooms and a storeroom, and, oh, what a storeroom it was. It held old trunks full of relics, funny hats, high-buttoned shoes, dresses, furs, and feathers, oh, such wonderful surprises in every corner. Every child should have such a storeroom of treasures."

(Excerpt from Mary's life-story written for her grandchildren in 1985)

We wonder if that was where Mary began her love of the arts and painting. Could those whitewashed walls have been the magic canvases responsible for unlocking her artistic skills? Certainly she turned often to creative activities throughout her lifetime: when in her classroom as a young teacher, for personal enjoyment, as a senior citizen student studying oil painting, and later as an arts teacher for adults: of flower arranging, leather tooling, copper etching and weaving. She learned how, and then taught them all!

Mary and fellow judge

She also became a highly respected fall fair judge at many of the fairs in Grey-Bruce, Huron and Wellington Counties in her last decades. In fact, she was a sought-after fine arts judge well into her late eighties. Quite an achievement for the little girl who drew on walls!

Mary's flair for anything artistic was reflected in her interior decorating ability, in the way she garnished her delicious meals, and in the seemingly casual way she allowed the beloved flowers in her garden to hold court on the coffee table or mantle. Flowers were a great love and she reveled in their beauty whether in her garden, in a painting or gracing her home.

It is quite fascinating that her efforts continued to give pleasure even after her death in September 2000.

In an estate auction after her home was sold, an interested observer, a Mr. Turner of Durham, Ontario, discovered some of her earlier works that had been propped for years in a back closet. These were works about which we'd all chuckled, then banished, forgotten.

Not only was this private collector excited enough to buy 18 paintings, nine of which were framed, he was so moved that he convinced the curator of the Durham Ontario Art Gallery to mount a retrospective of her work, which was held in November 2002.

A painting of Mary's circa 1951: one of her beloved autumn scenes

In the publicity Mary was described by the gallery as: *A unique artist due to her lack of formal teaching in art styles and brush work, but able to paint landscapes and animals such as ducks with great skill.*

Little Mary would have been so surprised, and, oh, so proud, as we, her children, were.

Progress

In 1911 the first telephones became fixtures in these farm homes. What an exciting boon to the community!

Now the farmers' wives could do some visiting back and forth without having to saddle up the horse and cutter or wander over the meadows to see each other. Each shrill, distinctive ring of longs and shorts would alert the whole line to the fact that people they knew were trying to chat with each other. The world was indeed shrinking just a tiny bit.

And what an exciting new activity for the four sisters! They realized it was such fun to listen in on the conversations of other folks on the same circuit. Soon they could recognize each specific ring, and if curiosity got the better of them and no one saw them, they would carefully pick up the receiver, try not to giggle or breathe too noisily, and listen for interesting gossip. Their parents did NOT encourage this!

The Hillis home was a hub of activity.

Later, I remember many summer holidays spent exploring this exciting dwelling. It seemed to be far more mysterious and special than the small-town bungalow in which I lived with my family. Their kitchen had a pump that needed a good deal of priming before the fresh, cold water gushed out. That seemed pretty innovative to my brother Ron and me.

Was this really the same sink that our mother, Mary, had used when she threw out the water so our Aunt Jean would be safe? Was the huge wood stove the place where the buckets of water were heated? There even was a reservoir full of hot water at one side of the stove, just right for a quick cup of tea. How novel. Of course, at the time I didn't appreciate that heating a kettle there was not just a case of putting in a plug and turning on a switch.

And imagine having a small pantry next to the kitchen. Our modern home did not have one of those.

I was intrigued. Glassed-in cupboards above the counter were full of bowls, crocks, pots, and kettles of every description. And there were many blue and white enameled jugs and pails, just like some seen in antique shops today. There were huge, serious looking meat grinders, colanders, enormous spoons, rolling pins the size of small trees, and other unimaginable treasure hidden in the cupboards below.

One could step down into a back kitchen, too, where the wood was stacked high, and where other unusual objects would catch my eye as I tried to figure out just how they were to be used. I was young enough during those visits to think that all of those fascinating new-to-me objects were quite romantic. However, from this standpoint, I would certainly not be prepared to exchange them for my dishwasher, freezer or microwave.

My enthusiasm about visiting Grandpa Hillis was somewhat tested by those necessary outside trips to the small out-house. This seemed like a giant backward step, especially if it was raining. And you can appreciate that I was very glad our holidays there were not in the frosty winter weather. Mind you, if the old Eaton's catalogue was there it did help to amuse us while we sat.

Nor did I enjoy the trips down into the dark cellar for provisions. It was another place I tried to avoid. If one went down about six steps, it was possible to reach over to a floating shelf and collect all manner of things; fresh pies, jams, roasts, or cheeses. That was no problem. And they were always yummy. It was cool and dark, but to be frank, rather scary for a little girl to have to stretch over that chasm to retrieve those delicacies.

I always kept my fingers crossed that I wouldn't be asked to go down a few steps more into the really spooky part.

Further into the cellar dank, dark rooms were waiting. There one could find bins of sand full of potatoes and root vegetables, deep crocks of pickles and sauerkraut, and even eggs in brine. These eggs sounded rather unappetizing to a 'town girl' who preferred 'fresh from the store' eggs, and refrigerators.

When we visited I usually scurried to other more interesting places, like the front parlor for example. I absolutely loved trying to play that upright organ. How wonderful to sit with little legs stretched to the max and pump, pump, pump, squeaking out rather unmusical sounds.

If those walls could have talked they might have told of the Sunday afternoons when Mary's family gathered around and sang old beloved hymns. When I hear the strains of '*The Old Rugged Cross*' or '*The Church in the Valley by the Wildwood*', I try to picture them sitting primly on the horsehair settee in their dainty dresses. Mary used to sing these hymns to us, often with a rather mystical expression flitting across her face. Memories....

This parlor was quite a formal room. Delicate doilies guarded pretty little tables, overstuffed furniture looked serious, and the family Bible held a place of honour beside the rocker. We remember hearing about what a marvelous meeting place it had been for their friends in days gone by. Mind you, they were quite likely drawn in by the gargantuan socials for which the Hillis family was noted, and possibly by the four comely daughters who lived there.

After the parlor became outmoded the door usually remained closed. The music now came from a grand Victrola near the huge new hot-air register in the dining-room floor. What a nice warm place to stand while using this fascinating object.

The melodies could soar either slowly or quickly, depending on how hard we cranked the handle. And it was even possible to turn the crank at just the correct speed so the words of yet another loved old tune could be jotted down, and then memorized.

Mary loved to tell us about how exciting it was when the first crystal radio arrived. She and her friends would cluster around the set, anxiously awaiting those first crackly sounds coming over the airwaves. It held court in a corner of the family dining room. Needless to say, this dining room, with its enormous chandelier over the table, became the hub of activity regardless of which generation was being entertained.

Mary told so many stories about their lives there. Spending money was scarce, but love and laughter was abundant. Store-bought toys were rarely part of their lives. However, mud pies decorated with flowers made pretty additions to wonderful make-believe tea parties. In a family of four girls, a ready-made cast of characters was always available to play house, have tea parties, and put on plays. They loved dressing up in their mother's dresses and hats, and what fun to pretend to be grown up ladies visiting each other. The drama of "pretending" was ever present.

Dress-up was not just for the girls. They even dressed their kittens (our mother's was a soft yellow bundle named Fluffy) in wee baby clothes and pulled them up and down the lane way in their wagons.

Family pet Rover hovered nearby and pet pigeons ate from their hands. All their horses had names, and quite often they wore pretty ribbons in their manes and sported sparkling bells for special occasions. Bessie and the other cows that they eventually had to bring from the back pastures every evening were like members of the family, too.

Having all of those animals to enjoy sounded quite wonderful. Who needed stuffed animals or mechanical toys!

School days

Mary first became a schoolgirl in Toronto. This unusual situation came about because her mother, our grandmother Hillis, needed an operation, and the closest available hospital was in Fergus, quite a distance away. How she must have hated to leave her infant baby Jean, only a few weeks old, and the other three children, too. And how difficult it must have been for her husband and the children to cope with life on the farm without her guidance and help.

Relatives were quickly called, and of course came to the rescue. Mary, our mother, was taken to stay with her namesake Aunt Mary, her Aunt Ella and her Grandmother Hillis in Toronto. It was a difficult time for all of them. Mary especially found the move frightening. Where did her quiet farm, and her kittens, her dog, the chickens and cows go? All of a sudden an overwhelming city surrounded her.

Rows and rows of houses were lined up side-by-side and people rushed everywhere. The sidewalks and streetcars were crowded and there were so many noises. At first she was lonesome and afraid. This was her very first experience of being away from home and it was scary.

Mary and her Aunt Mary with the special doll

Helping her adjust was her beloved Aunt Mary, a single business lady. Aunt Mary was wonderful, taking her to see the big stores, to Sunday school, to her friends' homes, and she even took photographs and let little Mary watch as she developed them in her dark room in the basement. This was in the infancy of photography so was quite an amazing activity for the little farm girl to experience. And it was quite an innovative hobby for Aunt Mary.

While there, a special doll was given to Mary. Its face was bisque and it wore a chocolate brown velvet cape lined with beige silk, and a matching bonnet edged in beautiful ecru lace.

It is still a stunning, blue-eyed, curly haired doll and continues to be treasured. However, when I was once allowed to play with her, I forgot to bring the beautiful cape inside. Alas, a sudden rainstorm drenched the garden and the rain caused the silk lining to become damaged and eventually disintegrate. I know my mother must have felt very badly, but I did, too, and still regret my carelessness.

Mary and friend with their dolls

The doll is a treasure, more so because the Dresden factories where these beautiful dolls were created were later completely destroyed in the war.

Mary was very, very fond of her Aunt Mary, who sadly developed double pneumonia, and died while Mary was living with them in Toronto. It was a very upsetting experience for Mary. She was anxious when the doctor came to visit, and spoke later about how she knew instinctively that her loved aunt had died even before being told.

Aunt Mary, a 44 year-old single lady, must have been a special woman of the times. Having a hobby of photography was quite a modern thing to do in 1913, and because of her creativity we have many photographs of the sisters, their parents, and their friends.

Mary Hillis, July 1870 – May 1913

She left her entire estate of $2,012.29 to Wilson, Mary's father. It consisted of two pieces of real estate, one, lot 120 on the east side of 17th St. in Etobicoke, and the other lot 4677 in York Co., a promissory note of $526.65, $1000 in insurance and funds in the bank. It is rather surprising that she would have such holdings in 1913.

Women were not considered to have much financial expertise at that time, so Mary must have been quite a progressive woman. Unfortunately we have no records of her working life. Little Mary has left an account of the long solemn train journey taking her aunt's coffin back to Hanover. What a sad voyage that must have been. Aunt Mary's funeral was held at the family homestead, with burial at Hanover Cemetery.

Other relatives cared for Mary's sisters while their mother was ill. Beatrice stayed with Aunt Polly in Port Elgin and baby Jennie with her Grandma Switzer, but big sister Florence stayed on the farm.

It is hard for us to believe that nine-year-old Florence would be left at home saddled with the responsibility of having to cook and help her father. Cows had to be fetched from the pasture, hens had to be tended, eggs gathered and meals had to be prepared. But nine-year-old Florence was a natural. She was easily capable of handling all of these activities and she managed them admirably. She loved farming and in fact, many years later she became the proud owner of the homestead. Her intuitive homemaking skills were obvious, her expertise was exceptional and she thrived on being a farmer's wife.

When the girls were all home again after their mother's illness, they daily had to walk two miles to the small schoolhouse where the big boys stoked the wood stove each morning. During the school day the little children assimilated many important lessons while they listened to the older ones. Those wee ears were always open as they busied themselves creating forms and figures with toothpicks and dried peas that had been soaking in water overnight. So much information was absorbed, remembered and tucked away in their minds for future reference.

Was listening to the older children recite poems where the love of poetry began?

Mary wrote wonderful poetry all of her life, with many of her poems accompanying gifts or cards to friends and family. Sometimes her verses were serious and touching and at other times they bordered on the absurd. As a family we would make up rhyming couplets or zany poems 'round robin style' while driving in the car, often breaking into gales of laughter at the ridiculous phrases that spontaneously erupted. When we were camping, Mother and I would create instant poems by the side of a lake while waiting for the men of the family to return with the catch of the day dangling from their fishing lines. Then what a feast we would have. The aroma of sizzling fish fresh from the lake is one of life's sweetest smells.

Perhaps the art of giving recitation was honed by listening to the older children in those early school years. This was a skill much appreciated by the community whose social lives revolved around school concerts and church socials. We must remember that these small settlements depended upon each other for just about everything. And although it is hard to imagine, movies, television, video games, Ipods, and computers had yet to be invented.

Mary won much praise for her eloquence. Many of her favorite recitations could still be rhymed off even when she was in her 90s. One particularly delightful selection required her to cover her teeth with her lips and lisp through a hilarious saga, all the while her hazel eyes flashing with glee. This selection never failed to generate tears of laughter even after we became grownups. Another one recounted the escapades of an unwise love and was called, 'Romance in a Hammock' How we used to coax her to tell just one more when we were children. There were sad ones too, such as one entitled, 'Hello Central, Give Me Heaven. Is My Mother There?'

The girls loved all aspects of nature and checked every minute seasonal change in the countryside while skipping the two miles to and from school. They enjoyed searching for the frogs in the creek, exploring wild strawberry patches, picking wild flowers and digging up the carefully hidden nuts gathered by the chipmunks. Once they even hid their shoes in a sandy hill en route so they could emulate their German schoolmates and go to school barefoot. I can just imagine them dusting their shoes and stockings off so carefully after school, putting them back on, swearing each other to secrecy, then continuing on to their home. That was one experience that their parents didn't learn about until the girls were all grown up.

They daily had to cross a river via a shaky footbridge made of wire and planks, and one spring day the water rose very, very high. At the end of the day their teacher carefully helped the children cross one at a time, and just as all were safely over, the wires snapped and the bridge was carried swiftly down the river. I remember having a picture on my bedroom wall when I was a child. It showed an angel helping two small children cross a swollen river, and I always associated it with the story of our mother's frightening experience that spring day. Angels surely must have been hovering nearby that afternoon.

As they grew older, big sister Florence drove them to school in their horse and cutter on cold, blustery days. Their father liked to braid the horse's mane with ribbons and tie sparkly brass bells into the harness. They looked so dashing as they sped along the road.

Mary, Beatrice, Jean, Florence and Old Nellie

In winter they loved to sail over the snow with bells jingling merrily. The sisters and their friends would pile into the cutter, snuggling under buffalo robes to keep warm and cozy.

Sometimes Old Nellie would dump them into a snowbank just to make the ride more exciting, but she always waited patiently until they dusted themselves off and climbed back in.

There were many tasks on the farm and the girls each took part. The nine cows had to be brought in from the pasture morning and night to be milked, and then the milk was put through the separator. It seemed like such a magical machine to me as a child but I imagine it became quite tedious to those who had to turn the crank each day. The barn cats got the skim milk, and the cream was put in large cans to be gathered in a cream truck twice a week and taken away to make butter. However, they did keep enough to make butter in their own churn. This was a favorite time for Mary because her mother would recite poetry and sing while they worked together. Eggs needed to be collected and the ducks, geese and chickens had to be fed. Helping in the fields meant that they sometimes had to pick stones to help clear fields for planting, but picking fresh carrots or puckery rhubarb was much more fun.

When we, who were brought up in towns and cities think about it, it seems as if they had to work extremely hard. But they grew to love life and each other, and it was a very happy home.

There was a large wild raspberry patch up in the bush, and when the berries were ripe, the girls took their pails and their lunch and off they went to pick those succulent morsels. And they were delicious. Naturally, they had to try a few, just to be sure! But the girls would always try to keep one eye on each other, so that no one ate too many berries, and so they each had brimming pails to take home. Twelve quarts was an average picking and their mother, our Grandma Hillis, would preserve as many as one hundred quarts of those berries every year.

They sold many, many pails of those fresh berries for which the ladies in town were happy to pay ten cents a pound. Mary was so proud of her first fountain pen, purchased with money she had made this way.

The girls helped their neighbours and their Grandma Switzer pick cherries and black currants, too. And how they loved to stay for meals after their work was done. Those neighbours who lived across the fields became so very special to the girls and were just like loved and treasured aunts.

Since there was no indoor plumbing, alternate arrangements were necessary in order to have a bath. A large boiler was placed on the woodstove and filled with rainwater from a cistern. When it was warmed just enough on the stove, a big tub was brought into the kitchen from the nearby woodshed. Then the youngest child bathed first. Down the line it went till all four were scrubbed clean, and then dried by the fire. Their flannelette nightdresses had been warmed by the woodstove, too. Can you imagine how cozy the children felt when they had pulled them over their heads and snuggled into them? Evening prayers were always said, hugs exchanged, and the four girls trooped happily off to bed, following the flickering glow of the coal oil lamp held aloft by big sister, Florence.

Were they remembering the taste of those juicy berries as they climbed the stairs to bed? Perhaps that day they had been sliding down the bush hill, climbing trees or looking for wildflowers in the woods. If it was wintertime they might have been rolling in the snow, making angels or funny snowmen families. They loved to toboggan when they fairly flew down the hills, the closest they could come to the mode of flying that was still being perfected. All of the times they spent together, whatever the season, was joyful. Being alive was wonderful fun in their comfortable farm home.

The seasons and years marched along by one, and the girls did too, all growing into pleasant young women and delighting in each stage of their lives. Lively singsongs around the organ in the Victorian parlor became favorite activities with their teenaged friends as they became older.

Many summer socials were held when the young men in attendance vied for a turn to crank the icecream maker and show their brawn. And winter fun usually included toffee pulls and high-jinks. I suspect that there must have been many walks through the woods as well, enjoying the beautiful land and each other's company.

Harvest time was a very special time for the whole community as grain was cut, gathered and threshed from the straw. First the grain was stooked in the fields, in readiness for the arrival of a dozen or more men from the area who were needed for the threshing. This activity took several days to complete, and was a wonderful time of togetherness. The wives also followed the thrashers during harvest, and even brought their children. It was a particularly joyful time for the girls when they were little.

I imagine as youngsters they and their friends piled into the attic playground to dress up, and share their games and their belongings. Undoubtedly just as soon as they were old enough to be helpful they were pressed into action in the kitchen too.

Dozens of pies, biscuits, muffins, and cakes were prepared. Steaming bowls of mashed potatoes, vegetables and meat appeared. Hungry appetites were appeased, and everyone enjoyed the socializing that flowed around the groaning table. It was a hectic time, but oh, how everyone loved it. Friendships formed then lasted their whole lifetime.

I have often wondered if the farm country habit of having several desserts at the evening meal was a direct result of all those many delights that found their way to the harvest table. Certainly, the love of baking was instilled in Mary and her sisters, and they all produced superb delicacies at the drop of a hat.

A very special time during our annual summer vacation with Grandpa Hillis was when we crossed the fields to visit again with those same folks who had helped bring in the harvest much earlier. Our mother became a child again, and the lively chatter of these dear friends made us blink with awe at their joy in being together.

Fast-forward to the year 1997 when Mary was celebrating her 90th birthday. Mary Fleming, the little daughter of one of those families joined in the birthday festivities remembering those times when our mother had been her very special babysitter. How wonderful to see the warm affection that being together gave both of them.

Mary Fleming Schenk and Mary Hillis Belfry

Following the birthday party Mary Fleming Schenk penned some thoughts about their families and the important bond between them. She recounts:

"*The Hillis family had been helping my young bachelor father care for his three step-brothers before he married our mother, so she as a new bride stepped into the love and friendship of Maggie and Wilson Hillis. The years were precious between them.*

The four Hillis girls were older and baby-sat sister Anna and me. Before we even started to school we could already make it across the fields to their farm. One day when we thought we had missed all the perils like fences to climb, stray cattle or horses we finally made it to the last gate. Then a huge African goose with a neck at least THREE FEET long reached for us. We had to cling to the fence till they could come and rescue us. When someone asked me why we called her "Aunt Maggie" she answered, "They call me Aunt because they love me I guess."

"And we did."

I can still see Mrs. Fleming's round shining face as she opened the screen door for our annual visit. Her face glowed, her gray bun bobbed on the back of her head, and her smile was at least a mile wide. Great hugs, and kisses and a whistling kettle set the tone for the day. What more could good friends ask for?

Mrs. Fleming's 80th birthday party! Back row left Jean 2nd, next Florence. Second row from post, Mary, and Beatrice, far right, Mrs. Fleming bottom left

Each fall after threshing Mary and her sisters stuffed their mattresses with fresh, sweet smelling straw. How inviting those mattresses were. At first they were always so full and high that chairs were needed so they could climb up onto their mountainous beds. Up the girls scrambled. What fun to jump up and down in those high puffy cloud-like mattresses. Gradually the straw settled down, as did the girls, and off to dreamland they would drift in their cozy nests.

At night before they went to bed their mother gathered them around her rocking chair, and read stories from the Bible. Those stories really stayed with Mary, and she continued reading her Bible all her life. Many of her favorite verses were memorized and became her constant companions for life.

The Bible gave her strength and wisdom and she continued to cherish it always. She was involved in Church activities, Mission Band, Women's Missionary Society, and Women's Auxiliary all her life. In her twilight years one could usually find her Bible, her diary and a book of poems beside her favorite spot to sit.

Winter Fun

Winter was long and cold in those days, and must have seemed especially so because central heating was still not part of their creature comforts. And their long prickly stockings and bulky underclothing were anything but stylish. The sisters simply hated them, but had to agree that the extra layers really did keep them toasty and warm. Their house had a furnace, but this did not send warmth into all parts of the house. Nor did the warmth from the kitchen woodstove even begin to reach those frosty bedrooms. They were so cold in their upstairs rooms that they usually dressed under the covers. When I had to do that on camping trips, it seemed like a lark. However, I don't imagine it would seem like such a delightful thing to do as a daily necessity.

The girls loved decorating their annual Christmas tree, with it with paper chains and long strings of popcorn, the ones that didn't get munched along the way. Strings of cranberries added bright colour and a big white bell always hung on top. Then stockings were hung beside the tree. Their mother always tied sparklers on the tree, too, which were lit on Christmas night. This sounds like a dangerous thing to do, and Mary said she often wondered why they never burned the house down. Perhaps this was a custom that Grandmother Hillis brought from her own German background.

I thought of this custom when on our honeymoon in a charming Austrian village that Christmas. A towering tree stood in the hotel dining room adorned with what seemed like hundreds of tiny candles. At a given time in the evening the candles were lit, and then all of the guests, Austrian, Canadian, Swedish, and German joined hands to form a circle and sing Christmas carols around the tree. It was a very special time but I, too, worried about the flames and did sneak a peek at the door in case a quick exit might become necessary. No doubt adequate precautions had been taken.

On Christmas morning the small Hillis girls were wide eyed waiting to see what Santa had put in the stockings. There was always a big orange in the toe, some hard Christmas candy -- the ones with flowers in the middle -- and some tasty nuts. Then there was always a special gift. Mary's most cherished gift was a ring with a ruby stone. How she loved it. She wore it constantly until she was in high school. Unfortunately it slipped off her finger one day when she was helping her father get hay from the mow. What a disappointment. It was not replaced until she was eighteen and received an amethyst ring that had been her beloved Aunt Mary's.

Their big brick farmhouse was located on a rise at the end of the long driveway. This home was a favorite place for the young people of the neighbouring countryside to congregate. Likely knowing that there were four winsome girls, and a mother renowned for her hospitality and delicious baking had something to do with the popularity of that Hillis home.

Usually wintertime included skating on a rink created in one of the fields, but twice a year they had a huge sleighride party. One of the neighbouring fathers went about the area gathering all of the young people with his sleigh and team of horses and then off they trotted to a nearby old mill.

While the older boys cleared the snow off the ice, the others gathered sticks for a bonfire. This was most welcome when toes and noses got nipped by the cold, or when they needed a rest after whirling on the ice. When cheeks were rosy and legs tired enough, they returned to the Hillis home singing their hearts out. There, taffy was ready to be pulled, and each tried to see who could pull hard enough to have the whitest taffy. Everyone knew that the harder you pulled the whiter it became, and oh, it was so delicious! Hot chocolate, huge plates of sandwiches, and singing ended the evening, and then off they went to the tune of the tinkling sleigh bells.

Mr. Fleming and Grandpa Hillis would go to the Neustadt Dam and saw huge blocks of ice from the 16-inch-deep frozen pond. Then they packed them into the sawdust in a special ice house. When the hot summer months arrived, the ice would be chipped and packed between a wooden tub and the metal liner in which there was a mixture of sugar, eggs, cream and milk. Handfuls of salt were added to the chopped ice, the lid was clamped on and a paddle inside the metal container was turned very hard for about a half an hour. When it became too hard to turn, they knew that ice cream was ready to eat. Mary Fleming remembers that the Hillis family made pink ice cream and they were all very impressed. Our supermarket ice cream would never be a match for this!

Another special community activity was the Box Social. Each girl prepared a tasty lunch and put it in a decorated box of her own making, which would then be auctioned off with much hilarity to the highest bidder. Auctioneers were fast-talking entertainers who urged the gallant young men to be bold and bid up for dinner with the girl of their dreams. After all the boxes had found new owners the successful purchaser could share the contents with its creator as well as take her home,

Mary, aged 15, and her dog

I imagine that a few well chosen clues about size, shape or detail were sometimes dropped into conversations in hopes the right purchaser would make the winning bid, but I have heard that occasionally the evening did not end quite they way things had been planned.

We appreciate that their lives were not easy, but this did not keep them from enjoying gleeful times. Industry and enthusiasm were integral to their success and happiness. And great dollops of love surely made a difference.

While the Hillis family settles into their lives in this rich farming community, we will wander down the road and across a concession to the Saugeen River where another family is about to enter our story.

The Hillis Family: Wilson Thomas Hillis and his family, Margaret Switzer Hillis, Jean, Bea and Mary Hillis

The Switzers

From the rise of the Hillis farmhouse one could see the Rocky Saugeen River meandering through the countryside in the distance. That very river had been part of the *highway* taken by Wilson Hillis's wife Margaret's forefathers when they crossed the country to claim Lot 17, Con 1 in 1850, and began their family history in this part of the Queen's Bush in Southern Ontario. It was a rugged, unpopulated area at that time. But they had been attracted to the land by the lure of a free grant of 50 acres with option to purchase additional acreage if requirements were fulfilled.

The Switzer family, later to include six daughters and four sons, made part of their trip along the Rocky Saugeen by boat in 1849. This must have been a difficult journey. Margaret's father, Benjamin, a small child in arms, was carried by his father, Benjamin, for whom he was named, during this rather daunting adventure. When this same Benjamin Switzer was in his 83rd years and the oldest Orangeman in the area, an article about his life and the settlement of Hanover was published in *The Hanover Post.* Written by a Mrs. E. C. Taylor, it tells the story of this pioneer family and some of their experiences as early settlers. These excerpts are taken from that historic interview of 1931.

These anecdotes about our ancestors allow us to glimpse the monumental task faced by pioneers.

Benjamin's parents (Benjamin: b 1809, Ireland and Mary Leonard: b 1817, Ireland) came to this country from Limerick in Ireland and settled in West Gwillimbury Township, near the town of Newmarket, Ontario. This is where Benjamin, the first-born son of their ten children, first saw the light of day on May 24, 1848.

When he was about a year old his parents moved into the backwoods and laid claim to a 50 acre homestead on the banks of the Saugeen, about three miles from the small, struggling hamlet of Hanover, Ontario.

There were no gravel roads in those by-gone times. In fact, there were no roads at all. The family had to walk along a narrow path winding through the dense forest, *guided by hatchet marks on the trees marking the right trail. (*These hatchet marks were called blazes and from this activity the expression "blaze the trail" has been added to our Canadian lexicon). *Farm implements had to be carried on their backs along with all their household goods.*

Settlers were most welcome and when a new family moved into the neighborhood everyone in the area came to assist in building the new home. The first house Benjamin has any recollection of was a one-story log shanty about 18 feet by 24 feet with a roof of split cedar clapboards.

The fireplace was built of clay, straw and sticks, and when these became dry and baked hard they were very good.

Most of the furniture of that first home was home made. The seats were a slab, with the flat side up and supported by four sticks, one in each corner, while the table was made of two wide slabs, fastened side by side and held up in the same way.

The article goes on to say that even at 83 years of age Mr. Switzer still walked into town each afternoon to visit the post office and greet his many acquaintances with his usual cheery smile. He played an important role in the town, serving more than 25 years on the former Methodist church board. He spoke of his delight in seeing that sleepy hamlet grow from a blazed trail through the bush bordered by very few shanties to become a paved thoroughfare to one of the leading manufacturing towns in Ontario.

In order to fully appreciate the lives of those relatives and their impact on this new country, we need to take some giant steps back several centuries to Europe where we believe our earliest connection of this Switzer family began.

The Rhineland Pfalz

This verdant, picturesque region in southwest Germany has France as a neighbour to the south and west, and the Rhine River and her tributaries to the east. A fertile valley, it has miles and miles of rolling vineyards. Historical records show that this region was under Roman occupation in 406 AD, annexed by Franconian nobleman Asso in 764 and under Charlemagne until 834. History tells us that it was frequently being pulled between French, then German forces no doubt because of its strategic location near the Rhine River, its good soil and its fair climate suitable for producing succulent crops. It was the first area to harvest early potatoes in Germany.

Today hillsides are crowned with castle fortresses, and small villages dot the Winestrasse that dissects the valley. Townsfolk take pride in their flower-bedecked windowboxes, thatched roofs and charmingly decorated homes. It is a part of the country steeped in traditional values where industrious families have been tending vines and raising families for centuries

However peaceful it may seem now, as history recounts, the border between these two countries was often under conflict and frequently redrawn depending on which power had the upper hand. After Martin Luther had taken a stand against the corruption of the Roman church at Wittenberg and arranged for the Bible to be translated into the German language, many families felt more comfortable following this less rigid form of worship.

During this time the term *Protestant*, which in the beginning meant 'protesters', originated at nearby Spires. It was so named for its many church spires but we know it now as Speyer.

Worms was another nearby large town where people preferred to worship with less formality, unlike the Roman Catholic form of worship.

In general, the Germans populace enjoyed more religious freedom than had been allowed for many years. But freedom of worship was not a universal right.

At Strasbourg in Alsace to the south, the Edict of Nantes of 1685 revoked the right of Protestants to both religious and political freedom, giving rise to a general feeling of unrest. Hence, many fled northward to the Rhineland where they felt their acquired rights would be respected.

Gradually more German worshipers chose the less rigid format. Unfortunately they suffered repeated attacks from the armies of Louis XIV who were intent on driving them out because of their religious habits. Truth to tell, the armies also coveted those rich, fertile lands and Louis craved the power that would be his with these farms in his possession. In the face of these problems the local German farmers became quite uneasy.

This area now recognized as the Rhineland Pfalz is still a fertile haven and continues to be sought after, although it is now tourists who seek its pleasures. Every year in late summer the countryside is gilded with glorious vineyards and the villagers celebrate their joy in yet another successful harvest.

Grape arbors crisscross main roads, wine "guts" are liberally scattered along the way to welcome visitors, and luscious fruits and vegetables take center stage in the local markets.

The Winestrasse or Wine Road begins at the French border town of Wissembourg and rolls through the beautiful German countryside for eighty kilometers.

Should you be fortunate enough to be there on the last Sunday of August, you would find this main road closed to vehicular traffic for the day. Then the whole world it seems takes to bicycles and rides from town to town, sampling the local wines and enjoying the launch of another vintage year.

At that dark era of history when our forefathers were striving for survival, it is unlikely that they could have imagined such joie de vivre in their beloved land. Among those who fled north from France and Switzerland were people called Schweitzer (meaning a Swiss, or person from Switzerland). It is our belief that these Schweitzers, whose name was gradually changed to Switzer, were the forefathers of the legions of Switzers who have survived and spread to many corners of the world. Noted but not proven by researcher Katherine Morningstar is the theory that Ludwig Schweitzer, a wealthy landowner in either Germany or Switzerland and born in the 1600's was the granddaddy of this whole tribe. Researcher Robert Switzer cites an old appraisal book of 1686 that says Ludwig Schweitzer was listed as the highest taxpayer in the area at that time.

Given this information, along with many other references in print and on the Internet, we will attempt to chronicle the activities of some members of this large family.

Our hope is that we can follow our own forefathers' exodus from Germany, first to England, then to Ireland, and eventually to our great-grandfather who built his homestead on the banks of the Rocky Saugeen River. There will be many twists and turns to this tale, not unlike the circuitous route that was followed in actuality those many generations ago. And there are likely just as many versions of this story, told around other crackling fires on cold evenings, or recounted by family member to relatives both near and far. Settle back. It is quite a fascinating saga.

The Switzer Connection

Johann Jacob Switzer (sometimes called Hans Jacob), son of Ludwig, was born around 1623 in the small town of Assenheim, Pfalz am Rhein. He was later conscripted into the army but was able to avoid action by hiding out in the thick forests, possibly living in covered wagons, but was back in the village of Bad Durkheim and working as a vineyard worker by April of 1647.

Through his industry he became a foreman and, with the stability of a more responsible position, decided to seek a wife.

Jacob became interested in Eva, the beautiful daughter of Michael Renner, Chief Magistrate of Assenheim, and the feeling was reciprocated. Her father also was pleased to welcome him as a suitor for his beloved daughter. The Court in Assenheim was re-established on April 30, 1647 and Jacob was invited to the formal proceedings of this happening by the invitation of Eva's father.

Eva and Jacob were married in 1650. The Lutheran Church Register at Bad Durkheim has the following notation:

On the 22nd of January 1650, Hans Jacob Schweitzer of Rheingoeheim and lead hand at Bad Durkheim was married to Eva, the endowed, legitimate daughter of Michael Renner, former Scultheiss of Assenheim.

Records tell us that Reverend Michael Mohr officiated at the ceremony. How amazing that, more than 350 years later, we are thinking of them, and trying to imagine what they were like. Quite likely the last thing on their minds was what an impact their commitment would have on so many of us these long generations later. No doubt they expected to share their lives until they reached 'a ripe old age'. However, researcher Claudette Filiputti believes that Eva died in childbirth along with her first-born child in 1657. Other researchers feel that the son lived and was cared for by others.

Stumbling blocks abound when following these families because of their practice of giving sons a religious name, such as Johann, and frequently naming the first son after his father, thus creating confusion when tracing their lineage. Further to this, the names Hans and Johann seem to have been interchangeable at that time. Consequently, Johann Jacob was alternately referred to as Hans. This family used the prefix 'Ye Elder', a frequent term for the first-born son. Later records also list the term 'Ye Younger". To a degree this does help to define their lineage more accurately.

However the similarity in sons' names has contributed to a great deal of confusion for those of us who are trying to follow specific Switzer lines. Be that as it may, we do feel that this gentleman is very likely our first forefather. Wesley B Switzer (***The Irish Palatines, rev 1993***) tells us that Eva's death in 1657 made Jacob (to be known as Hans Jacob the elder) lonely and unhappy. He had enjoyed married life for seven years and he did not like living alone. After a respectable period of mourning was observed, he began courting Elisabeth Kesselring, the daughter of the Schulteiss of the neighbouring village of Ellerstadt. They married in April 16, 1658. A child born to these parents was Johann Jacob the younger, b. 1658 (and quite probably the same Jacob Switzer of Courtmatress who was buried in Rathkeale, Ireland in 1746). Later Hans Dieter and Hans Nicklaus were also born to this family.

Peace reigned for some years during which time Hans Jacob the Elder was appointed to the Court of the village of Assenheim, which was a lifetime appointment. They were an important part of the community and grew in prosperity.

Jacob's son, Hans Jacob, the Younger, married **Anna Maria** around 1680 and their first child, **Hans Michael** ,was born in 1681. His brother, **Hans Christopher,** arrived in 1686. Four other sons were born to these parents later but we will try to narrow our focus and concern ourselves mostly with these two pivotal brothers.

As we have heard, a peaceful existence was not to last in that area of Germany. Its rich agricultural land was highly coveted. The very lives of those who lived there were being threatened by marauders, and frequent attacks from the armies of the south made life difficult for them.

No doubt the townsfolk of Assenheim were becoming uneasy. Was there a safe haven in other lands? We can picture them quietly weighing the possible problems they could meet in a new country and having to master a new language.

The anxiety of having to leave their family and loved ones, as well as all the familiar haunts of their homeland must have made their decision all the more difficult. What a choice to have to make.

Around this time the British government was most interested in encouraging the Palatines to consider emigration to the American colonies. With this in mind a "Golden Book' designed to woo the hardworking peasants of southern Germany was circulated among them. The 'land of milk and honey' descriptions sounded quite wonderful. Bread was to be available until they could produce their own, and many were indeed anxious to leave the problems at home for this new adventure. Henry Z. Jones **(The Palatine Families of Ireland**) believes that the adventurous spirit of these Germans who became interested in taking the risk was one of the reasons that they succeeded so well.

The winter of 1708-09 was a particularly brutal one with heavy frost still deep in the soil well into late April. We are told that even the Rhine River froze from the

North Sea to the Alps. Grape harvests were destroyed and Hans Jacob the Younger's sons became unemployed. Many anxious hours must have been spent searching for a solution. Certainly, the glowing campaign from Britain must have sounded like an exciting answer to their problems. What an opportune solution for adventure and success.

Records Tell Us

Numerous researchers have described the departure of these Palatines as they were called. The journey down the Rhine from the Pfalz area (known as the Palatinate) to Rotterdam and the sea took from four to six weeks in those days. Many families began making plans to leave their beloved homeland via this route. What would they need in their new lives? How could they leave treasured objects and beloved family members behind?

Soon many villagers began the river trip. We can only imagine the sorrow this must have caused in the little village of Assenheim.

Johann Schweitzer's sons, 28-year-old Michael with his wife Dorothea, parents of sons (Johannes Antonius, 1704, aged 2 years, and 6 months old Johannes 1709), and 23-year-old Christopher must have had many sleepless nights. They must have anguished over the wisdom of their decision to seek new lives. And they must have been concerned about leaving their parents, siblings, and other loved ones behind.

Several parties of German Protestants left their homeland via Rotterdam and the Switzer brothers were on the third sailing.

3. Nicholas (probable sons of above)						Killeneen
STROUD John Strouch	3rd	aged 30, wife, 1 son, aged 2.	Lutheran	Husbandman & Vinedresser	Yes	Philipina Strouch, probably his widow Killeheen
SWITZER 1. Michael Schweitzer 2. Johann Christopher Schweitzer	3rd 3rd	aged 28, wife, 2 sons, aged 6 months, 2. aged 23, alone.	Lutheran Lutheran	Husbandmen & Vinedressers	Yes Yes	Courtmatrix Courtmatrix
TESKEY 1. Jacob Teskey 2. Jacob Jun .3. Solomon (son of above)	2nd	aged 50, wife, 2 sons, aged 16, 20.	Lutheran	Turner	Yes Yes	Killeheen Killeheen Killeheen
TETTLER/DETLOR						

This information is taken from an article entitled **Palatine Families on the Southwell Estates 1709-12 to 1720** by Patrick J. O'Connor, reproduced in *The Irish Palatine Association Newsletter, No. 2 December 1991*

Religious concerns were on the mind of Queen Anne of England at this time as England was also going through a crisis between the Roman Catholic believers and those who had changed their religion to the Church of England. 'Good Queen Anne' and some of her commissioners felt that these German Protestants would strengthen the anti-Roman-Catholic feelings in Britain. Consequently she sent the English Navy to Rotterdam to ferry these Palatine people across the channel to Blackheath, near London.

Records of the day (researched by Patrick J. O'Connor in his book ***People Make Places: The Story of the Irish Palatines*** and ***The Palatine Families of Ireland*** by Henry Z. Jones) reaffirm that Michael and his family were on the third sailing from Rotterdam, as was his brother Johann Christopher. About 3,000 of the travellers were sent directly to America, and many more went to England and eventually Ireland.

By the summer of 1709 there were some 1300 Germans waiting in rather temporary settlements along the Thames at St. Catherine's, eager to be moved into new communities.

The Southwell Settlements

Through Queen Anne's efforts Sir Thomas Southwell, a former British baronet who had moved to Ireland some years before, was encouraged to grant tenancies to these Palatine settlers, allowing them to work and live at Castlematrix, Killeheen and Ballingrane near Limerick. As they were experienced husbandmen, vinedressers and weavers he readily agreed to her request.

On August 8th this group travelled across the English countryside by wagon to Chester, a distance of 120 miles. From there a schooner took them to Dublin, which was a 24- hour journey.

What an eternity it must have seemed to these travellers who had left home many weeks before.

Enumeration details at St. Catherine's south of London in 1709 tell us that there were 48 of those German families. This number was augmented by additional families in the next few years. In 1720 there were 103 Palatine families listed as residing with Sir Thomas Southwell at Castle Matrix, Co, Limerick. The hope was that these German Lutherans would bring their remarkable agricultural skills to the region, and marry with the local populace.

Queen Anne felt that creating a Protestant stronghold in this otherwise Catholic area would give positive strength to her Empire. Good working conditions and relief from taxes made the offer quite attractive and many chose to settle in that part of Ireland. Generous financial terms were put in place too so that each Palatine family would receive an annual grant of 40 shillings for seven years. Later, seven more years were agreed to and this allowance was raised to 624 Pounds and was to be continued for an additional 14 years on expiration of the former grant. No doubt this assistance was most welcome and helped the Palatines to flourish.

A few interesting facts have been unearthed about the Southwell Estates. It seems Castle Matrix was built circa 1410 by the FitzGeralds. Walter Raleigh, well known to history, received the freedom of the town in 1580 as a reward for ambushing some Irish who were trying to plunder an English encampment there. Raleigh also repaired the castle at Rathkeale following which the area was divided among the Spensers, Raleighs and Edmund Southwell. Raleigh, who had previously been in the Americas, gave some "Virginian Tubers" as a present to Southwell, who planted them in land around Castle Matrix. In 1610 these crops were distributed throughout the province of Munster. And so potatoes became a staple in Ireland. Could they have been some of the potatoes of which we have heard in the years to come?

Researcher Ken McDonald, the UK Internet contact from whom I received my invaluable Assenheim connections, mentioned that the first potatoes grown in Europe after Sir Walter Raleigh brought specimens home from America, were grown on the Southwell Estate. It gives pause for thought when we consider the devastation that Ireland suffered because of the dreadful blight of the potato crop in the mid 1800s.

The infamous Potato Famine which resulted had a significant effect on many lives. The virus caused the flesh of the potato to turn to a milky liquid, and because potatoes were a major crop, many hundreds died of starvation. Countless families who people our country were driven to America in search of new lives as a direct result of the dreadful famine that raced across Ireland. Many of our ancestors joined the trek to the new world partly because of this phenomenon.

These industrious German farmers settled enthusiastically into life in Ireland. Their first crops were flax and hemp from which fine linen and coarse cloth were produced in a Rathkeale factory. Kitchen gardens were planted, and then wheat and orchards. Their method of planting potatoes was to place them in ridges rather differently than how crops had been planted to this point. It became a popular planting concept and was later to become the chosen method used by all Irish farmers. They also used more sophisticated planting methods using horses and tilling tools allowing them to plant faster, thus producing larger crops

A vegetable called "German cabbage" was also introduced (***The Irish Palatines*** by Dudley Levistone Cooney, IPA publication). He says, *"When growing up I was introduced to German cabbage or sauerkraut when visiting my grandfather. It is an acquired taste, and I liked it."* One assumes that this vegetable was really cabbage but cooked using vinegar, salt and spices in the German tradition.

Imagine my own surprise when driving in the environs of Assenheim. I realized that I could smell the strong aroma of cabbages as we passed rich, green fields of produce. Could I really smell them or was I transported back to my childhood summers when we had sauerkraut on our visits to Hanover, Ontario? I am not sure why this happened but it was only in the one area near the village. Perhaps recent harvesting caused the aroma, or it could have been just an overactive imagination.

Many of these settlers had up to 16 children, so these large families gradually spread into nearby communities. Adare, Rathkeale, and Ballingrane were some of the villages where they settled and reared families, and some also spread further into counties of Tipperary and Monaghan. They enjoyed this environment, they did teach their farming skills to the native Irish farmers by example, but intermarried most often within their own community, thus defeating one of the hoped for outcomes.

Often these marriages were arranged by families of young girls whose parents realized that properties would be enhanced if joined to that of a prosperous neighbour. It was not unusual for brides as young as 14 to marry but remain under the parental roof until they were 16, after which they would join their husband. Grooms, usually older, would have already established their homesteads, thus proving their worth. Marriages were not always arranged, and comely young lasses could and did easily attract suitors on their own.

Some of these new families lost sight of their Protestant ethics for a while and stopped attending church. However, John Wesley visited in 1758 and returned several more times to the area. He preached to many groups, admonishing them for their less than religious zeal, and finally most returned to their original beliefs. His lessons must have been taken to heart as we learn from the pages of history that some of Wesley's disciples including Barbara Heck from this area were instrumental in introducing the Methodist Church in America.

When driving through the Limerick area several years before starting this writing project we had just passed through the pretty village of Adare when we spotted a rather decrepit sign pointing down a lane to Castle Matrix. A bell went off in our minds. Wasn't that where the Switzer family came from? Being curious we decided to follow it.

At the end of the short road stood a crumbly edifice proclaiming its ancient heritage with its gray crenellated stonewalls and a timeworn facade.

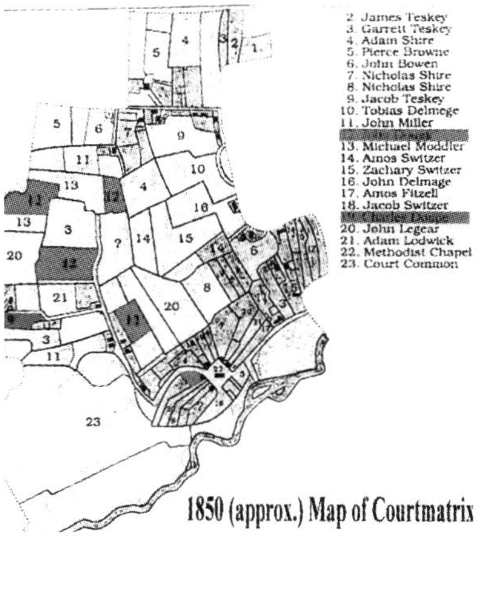

1850 (approx.) Map of Courtmatrix

Nearby were long, low buildings, accentuated by archaic windows, doors, and chimneys. Could these have been some of the dwellings where our forefathers lived? It was noted that the immigrant families were housed in low dwellings forming a square much like the buildings we saw, but confirmation that this was the site has yet to be proved. More research is needed here. Perhaps even another visit to Ireland. Jacob Switzer's property was # 18 near the Methodist Chapel on the green. His daughter Margaret married the architect Philip Heck who boarded with them, and this couple, along with Barbara Heck, helped to spread the Methodist's beliefs in the North America.

We believe now that the entrance we saw was a little used one from the old road. There is now a new road and a more imposing entrance leading to much larger buildings with similar crenellated walls and architectural characteristics. Researcher Ken MacDonald has a map of the area on his website showing both new and older roads in the area and it looks as if we entered by the back door, as it were. Quite likely the larger castle was the main dwelling in the time of our ancestors. In recent years the castle was purchased and refreshed by an American named Sean O'Driscoll and has been used as a hotel.

Similar to the main castle **Castle Matrix** **Outer buildings**

Switzer Family Development

This very large Switzer family has offspring now living in many parts of the world. They have worked hard, lived interesting lives, and many researchers and genealogists have documented their travels. We, too, are trying to unravel the information. Doubtless the link stretches from those first German Switzer settlers to our particular connection.

The whole Palatine saga that has captured the attention of people in many parts of the world over the years soon began to intrigue me, too. I wondered how I could have lived in France, a few hundred kilometers from the village of Assenheim in the 1960s, and not realized this is where one aspect of our family began? My brother Ron first learned of the Switzer foothold in Limerick while on a bus trip to Ireland. This was the first important link to our Switzer forefathers.

Then; diaries and notes left by our mother, Mary, after her death in 2000, started the ball rolling in my mind. My next source of information came from the Internet.

Many details unfolded about the exodus of the Palatine, and their struggles to find new homes. Soon fascinating information began pouring in. Each new search drew me further into the maze of details about the Palatines, their adventures, and the Switzers who were part of the story.

Gradually I read the names of families with whom the Switzers had lived, traveled and planted roots. I realized that many bore the same family names as classmates I had had, like Shires, and Brethors. Many of the people who had lived in the small town of Uxbridge, Ontario, where we grew up also had names like the St Johns, Rynards, Harmans, Lows and Cronsberrys, who had fled to Ireland, too. Slight spelling changes were apparent, but were still quite recognizable. Many other small Ontario towns and villages reflect these same names and backgrounds as well.

Along the way my search for information has led me to connect with many other interested individuals. As seekers and learners, valuable data has been shared via the Internet. Many new friends have most generously shared their enthusiasm and knowledge about the historic exodus from Germany, to Ireland and then to the New World of the Americas. Let us see if we can untangle some of the web our forefathers have created.

Back to the Beginning

One day on a Google search I came upon details of a 2004 visit some Palatine descendents had made to Bad Durkheim and Assenheim, Germany. This was the historic location where the first traces of our tribe had been unearthed. How fascinating! My interest was piqued. Carefully I noted the names and email addresses of some of the participants.

Maybe I could contact one of them. So, I clicked on Ken MacDonald's name and soon a floodgate opened and many new contacts appeared. Ken lives in England and his interest is through the Tesky family, some of whom married Switzers. Another person contacted was Terry Jackson from England, who turned out to be a second cousin. Amazing! Ken sent my query to several other researchers, and gave me the name of Monika Schöenbucher who still lives in Assenheim. Monika, although not of the Switzer line, had been equally intrigued by the drama of this family and was pivotal in organizing the Switzer tour of 2004.

While all of this material was swirling in my head, the fates were having a picnic. A reunion was being planned for those Canadians who had been involved in a NATO exercise a decade after World War II.

We learned that the towns of Longuyon and Marville in France where NATO's Canadian RCAF #1 Wing Base had been located (1955-1967), and Virton and Florenville in Belgium where many military personnel had lived during their deployment, were planning a reunion for those Canadians who had been part of the exercise. My husband Bill, as a recent military college and engineering grad, was posted to #1 Wing finishing his commitment to the RCAF as a Sabre pilot, and I, a Toronto teacher, had been 'on loan' there for two years to teach the children of the service personnel. We both had arrived at #1Wing during 1959. There we worked, played and traveled, together with fellow teachers, pilots, and nurses drawn from across Canada. We certainly were eligible to attend the reunion, and it sounded like a wonderful idea to return to our salad days.

The festivities were to be held over the Labour Day weekend of 2005. Were we interested? Yes, we certainly were. Reservations were quickly made and we looked forward to seeing the place where we had met, married and lived for four years.

This would be a perfect opportunity to revisit old haunts. And since it wasn't far away from the Rhineland-Pfalz area of Germany, perhaps we could visit the original village of the Switzer branch of our family tree to see the countryside from which they had sprung. Soon, via the internet, we found a suitable hotel in Bad Durkheim near Assenheim, as it seemed like a central location from which to do our family research.

This is where Monika Schöenbucher came into the picture. I innocently asked by email if it would be possible to visit the town during the late summer and hopefully fill in a few of the blanks in my research. I envisioned visiting the town offices to see if original documentation could be viewed, and perhaps acquire copies for my research. Her enthusiastic response came at once. She thought it would be wonderful, and despite plans that would take her out of the country (to Ireland in fact) during our visit she set the stage for a most memorable experience for the two of us.

And so in late August of 2005 we spent four delightful days exploring the area from our home-away-from-home at Hotel Pfalzer Hoff in Bad Durkheim. This centre,

now a well-known spa town, is a busy, bustling city amid the rolling vineyards. What a delightful spot to soak up the atmosphere, stroll, and absorb the cadence of the area.

Being inveterate tourists, we visited Speyer and the famous Dom, and Worms, where Martin Luther was reviled because of his beliefs. These cities with their famous cathedrals were certainly fascinating. But it was the small villages all garbed in marvelous masses of flowers, overflowing windowboxes, pretty gardens, and charming half-timbered buildings that most intrigued us.

Local architecture

As we explored we could see that the rich harvest was ready, the vineyards were groaning with luscious grapes, and the villages were festooned with the fruits of the season. Preparations were obviously underway for the annual wine celebrations, and we enjoyed wandering the streets of the cities and villages, driving through the pretty countryside, and picturing what it must have been like before industrialization shouldered in.

Assenheim, Germany

Then, very early on the last Sunday morning of August, as arranged by Monika, her father, Egon Fix, appeared at our hotel to be our tour host, and to take us to the 8:30 a.m. church service in Assenheim.

This was the day that the 80 kilometer road which winds through the countryside from the border of France and is known as the Winestrasse, was to be closed to vehicular traffic for the celebration of the year's vintage. Because of the road closures there was concern that we might not be able to get to their village, or get back to our hotel after our visit. Egon's knowledge of the area enabled us to deftly detour along back roads and short cut, thus avoiding the many roadblocks. Quite likely we would have been hopelessly lost had we tried to navigate the route by ourselves. Along the way we collected Marga, Monika's mother, in the nearby village of Rodersheim, before continuing to the Evangelical church, dated 1758.

Assenheim Evangelical Church, Assenheim Germany, erected 1789

We did not know quite what to expect, but what a moving morning it was. English-speaking folk from the church and community had been alerted and awaited our arrival. We were warmly received by friendly English-speaking and German parishioners, and were welcomed by the minister from the pulpit in both German and English. Our welcome was heartwarming and sincere and we were made to feel so very special.

What a wonderful feeling. It was especially poignant to sing 'Morning Has Broken' and recite the '121 Psalm' in German, and to feel the words deep inside. How fortunate we felt to be there.

Yes, we were among strangers, but the thoughtful townsfolk seemed delighted that we wanted to be among them, and treated us as returning family. Before leaving home we had taken a few German lessons but were certainly far from fluent. As luck would have it, we had practiced 'Morning Has Broken' with our tutor so were able to sing and understand the words reasonably well.

Our smattering of the language helped somewhat but the sincerity of these caring folks was very easily translated. The church itself glowed with rich wooden benches, curving choir stall and burnished wooden paneling on walls and ceiling. We have since learned that the wonderful old Geib-Orgel organ in the sanctuary is renowned. Artists from many places in Europe and North America come here to experience its rich sound and to give frequent concerts. Even a Canadian artist had presented a concert in the recent past. We marvelled at this unique instrument (installed in 1785) and were able to examine it closely after the service.

How very sad to discover later that this little village had not escaped the ravages of World War II. The following historical information regarding those years of strife is chronicled in documents given to us on our visit.

Elizabeth Zarate, a lovely lady whom we met that morning has thoughtfully translated several articles of interest for us since our visit and has kept in touch often by email.

Elizabeth Zarate and Bill Lynn at the Rathaus reception

Elizabeth's help has contributed greatly to our understanding of the historical background of this delightful area and we truly value her willing assistance and friendship.

Elizabeth translates:

During the war 1939/45 Assenheim was the most air-raided village compared to surrounding communities. Around the village many high explosive and incendiary bombs were thrown into the fields.

There were even very heavy mines that to some extent didn't explode. In the night of 9th to 10th August 1943 Assenheim was heavily ravaged by incendiary bombs. During this siege 23 brimming barns burned down completely. In most of the other premises the incendiary bombs could be extinguished. Fortunately, nobody was hurt.

On Monday, 19th March 1945, shortly before the Americans arrived, 6 persons were killed by fighter-bombers and one woman was mortally wounded. Numerous other persons were wounded as well. Several premises were considerably damaged. In the Evangelic church the parochial chair, the staircase to the pulpit and two seats were damaged by fire. Between 1939 and 1945, 146 men were drafted, 26 of them were killed and 11 are still missing. No prisoners of war returned.

It is a sad commentary on man's inhumanity to man! As we walked the streets of this picturesque village we tried to imagine the horror of living there during such difficult times.

Following the church service we took photographs of the church and some of the parishioners to mark the occasion and then all crossed the road to the Rathaus Town hall).

Assenheim Evangelical Church
1735 – 1887
Psalm 121

Parishioners in front of the historic Evangelical Church, 1789, Assenheim, Germany
Back left: Egon Fix
Centre Front: Marga Fix and Bill Lynn
Front right: Elizabeth Zarate

Historic beam from the year 712
Restored Rathaus in Assenheim

The inscribed beam can be seen on the right front of the Rathaus. There, carved on a corner post of this restored historic building, were names of some of the town officials from the early years. And among them was Tieter (Dieter to us) Schweitzer's name. He too was a son of Johann Jacob. Teiter and several other officials present at the original buildings' inauguration were city councilors at the time the Rathaus was dedicated. The date inscribed on the post was 1712 just a few years after our relatives had left for other shores! Records point to the fact that this man was a brother of Michael and Christopher, the two young men who carried Christopher's children down the Rhine River in 1709 in search of a more stable lifestyle.

It seems likely that Teiter made the decision to remain in the Assenheim community and eventually became a city father.

A warm gathering of friendly people awaited us in the reception rooms of the lovingly restored Rathaus. We were able to examine historic photos of early years, giving us a glimpse of a long-gone lifestyle. Were those sturdy pillars and huge beams in the reception rooms the ones that our forefathers helped to carefully place in the original building? Could they have known that people from many parts of the world would still care several hundred years later? Village records refer to the fact that much of the original building and effects were incorporated into the new building. Pride shone on the faces of these townsfolk. Their sparkling Rathaus was testimony to the determination of members of a small village that has survived in the face of many anxious moments over the centuries.

We were delighted to be greeted by so many friendly folk who shared their interest and knowledge of the past, their travel experiences in Canada, and above all, their enthusiasm for our search for our family roots. One friendly Switzer descendant even greeted me with *"Hello Cousin."*

The symbols on the town crest reflect the historic joining of two neighbouring village, Assenheim and Hochdorf. One prominent feature of the crest is a pair of eyeglasses. This symbol of wisdom and erudition was appropriate to use where magistrates deliberated about the community's welfare. It appeared carved in wood on the post from 1712 where the city fathers names appear. Over time this emblem began appearing on village fire extinguishers and hewn in stone and wood around the area. It also features in the demarcation line between the two joined communities, where initials were added, an HD for Hochdorf which looked toward one village and an A for Assenheim which pointed the other way. Elizabeth Zarate also helped by translating this explanation for us.

For the rest of the morning, the sincerity and interest of all of the townsfolk was palpable. We did appreciate that, although we were total strangers, our arrival had prompted their warm reception.

We were moved by the many thoughtful gestures and the enthusiastic reception. A gracious, official welcome by the mayor's representative was most touching. This was especially appreciated as we realized that he too had to take time from his own weekend plans to come to Assenheim and bring us greetings, certainly not what one would expect in our own land.

Bill Lynn and Margaret Belfry Lynn sign the register

Presentations and copies of our Switzer family historical genealogical data were made, along with a book about the village history, and a cookbook full of traditional recipes assembled by the women of the community.

Then we were invited to sign the town hall register. What a thrill! After sharing the delightful refreshments and bubbly, we thanked them for their generosity and said very fond goodbyes. Miles and years melted as we visited that morning. We felt as if we had been on a long journey and were being happily welcomed back home. What a feeling of kinship it gave us.

Our hosts for the day took us to their home after the official functions, and we enjoyed seeing family photos, being in their lovely home, and learning about and seeing their market gardening produce. We were even given some crunchy apples to take back to our hotel for later snacks. The fact that we did not understand each other's language was not a deterrent to communication. Marga and Egon offered true hospitality and we were very touched by their offer of a meal.

However, we felt that we should return to Bad Durkheim and let them enjoy a more relaxing afternoon. We were extremely appreciative of Monica, Marga and Egon's daughter and her efforts and organizational skills in working out the dynamics of this visit. Despite the fact that we were total strangers, she set in motion one of the most memorable mornings we could remember.

Egon returned us safely to Bad Durkheim where we were able to see and be part of the local celebration to officially present the 2005 vintage. Bicycles by the hundreds, bustling wine kiosks, and happy children of all ages filled the square and overflowed in all directions. What a marvelous party! What a joyful day it was!

Seeking information about long forgotten forefathers is sometimes a tedious task, but this was certainly a Red Letter Day for us! We were thrilled. The generosity of strangers can make such a significant difference. The commandment that asks us to "*Do onto others that which you would have others do to you*" comes to mind!

A common language need not be a requisite when people genuinely wish to help one another.

The beautiful Nuremberg angel Christmas tree ornament purchased while visiting that famous Kriskrindle Market many years ago is even more special after this very personal link to past patriarchs has been forged.

Now let us get back to the forefathers of the Benjamin Switzer family who were beginning to put deep roots into the soil near Hanover, Ontario.

From here on there are often differing opinions about the lineage of our Benjamin's forefathers. Different spellings appeared too as younger family members began to use the more anglicized spelling 'Switzer' instead of the old German Schweizer. Families were huge and many similar names and dates crowd the historical ledgers. Let's establish what we know of this family to this point:

Switzer Genealogy Data

The first few entries of this genealogical data are taken from Assenheim records we received during our visit. Additional data from The '*Palatine Families of Ireland' by Henry Z. Jones* has been included.

Familien in Hochdorf und Assenheim, by W Seelinger

Hans Jacob Schweitzer: b.1630 - d.1710, Assenheim Germany;
m. 1) **Eva Renner:** b.1623 - d. 22 Jan. 1657, m. 22 Jan. 1650, d/o Michael Renner, Schulteiss of Assenheim (1623-1630). Eva could have died in childbirth.
Hans Georg, b.1658 - d.19 March 1737
2) m. **Elisabeth Kesselring**, b.1625 - d.1686, Ellerstadt, Ger., m. 16 April 1658 in Ellerstadt, Ger., d/o Michael Kesselring, Schulteiss of Ellerstadt.

They became property owners in Assenheim and Hans Jacob was appointed to Assenheim Village Court 18 Nov, 1669, and held position for life.

Children from second marriage

1). Johann Jacob: b.1658, Assenheim - d.1734, Courtmatrass, Ireland, m. **Anna Maria**: b.1660 - d.1746 Courtmatrass, Ire., m. 1661

2). Niklaus: b. 1700 - d. 1746, Courtmatrass, m. **Maria Margarita Strebel** 1676

3) Hans Dieter: b.?? **-** d. 1748, m. **Maria Kath.** 1694 - 1741

4) Michael: b. 1681, Assenheim **-** d. 29.Sept.1768, Courtmatrix

5) Barbara: b. 26 Sept 1677, Deidesheim, Ger.

6).**Christopher:** b.1686.- d. 29 May1755, Courtmatrix; m. **Catherine Elizabeth Ruckle:** b.1720 , Ireland, d.12 May 1788, Parish Church, Rathkeale, Limerick, Ireland

Michael (#4) and **Christopher** (#6) were the two young men who traveled to Ireland on the third sailing in 1709.

Although Michael was undoubtedly a fond brother, and one who continued to play an important role in the successes of this extended family, we will relegate him to rather less important status in our personal family history. With luck this will allow us to separate our immediate relatives from the vast numbers of Switzers, and concentrate on finding our way through our own connection. Hopefully we will establish Christopher's lineage, as we believe that he is our patriarch. Sleuthing has found so many similarly named characters reverberating through the historical records that our heads are awhirl. No doubt they all would love to peek into these pages and/or get a toehold for posterity. However, a ruthless approach has been necessary.

The Ruckle Connection

It is appropriate here to mention a close family connection that appears and reappears through the lives of the Switzers. This is the Ruckle family. We note that Caspar Ruckle and our Switzer brothers were among the third party of Palatinates who sailed from Rotterdam in 1709 (***Irish Palatine Association Newsletter, Dec 1991*). These** brothers settled in Courtmatrix. Caspar Ruckle is listed as having sailed with his wife and child and settled in nearby Ballingrane. There was also a Caspar and family on the 6th sailing. Christopher did marry Catherine, a daughter of Caspar in 1720, but it is not clear to which family she belonged.

The following information on this family is found on a Ruckle website.

JOHN CASPAR RUCKLE/RUTTLE

The name Ruckle/Ruttle stands for strength and courage.
Family motto, "Der Lerr ist mein fels"
(The Lord is my Rock).
John Caspar (or Casper) was born in Germany.
He was said to have been with the 3rd party
of Palatines at St. Catherine's with wife and one child.
He was listed as age 49 at London, England in 1709.
John Roogall listed on 07/13/1715 as a Palatine family
in Ireland and on 09/29/1720 as head of a Palatine family
on the Southwell Estate. After 1720
the family settled at Ballinggrand in an
area known as Ruckle Hill and in later
years known as Fort View.

Of question are the many different spellings of the name Ruckle. It has been alternately written as Rutsel, Rigell, Roogall, but a Ruckle Family Bible has helped to confirm the that all of the variations refer to the same family (Ruckle family website), and the family was certainly well enmeshed in the lives of many of our Switzers. Ballingrane (Ballinggrand) was only a mile or so South West of Rathkeale and quite near the area called Courtmatrix, the main village settled by this first wave of Germans.

Courtmatrix, which is alternately called Courtmatress or Castle Matrix, reflected the German architecture and way of life with its neat, well cared for thatched dwellings built in a square around the commons. Twenty Palatine families were located there, and Christopher was listed as a freeholder there on July 13, 1715, as well as in 1720 and 1755. He was buried there 29th May1755. Martin and Elizabeth's large family takes us to the next generation

Children of Christopher Schweitzer and Catherine Elizabeth Ruckle:

1) Martin: b.1725 - d. 6 March 1796 (Ye younger), Freeholder at Courtmatrass in 1776 and Feb. 1783
m. 1) **Anna Barbara Legier**, b.?? - d. 15 May 1763, Rathkeale,
m. 3 April 1744

m. 2) **Catherine Kennedy**, b.1732 - d. 12 May 1788
2) John: b.1732 - d.1815; m. **Anna Maria Guier**, 9 March 1753
3) Tobias: b.1733 - d.1810; m. **Dorothy Shire** 19 November 1754. There were several other Switzer/Shire marriages
4) Peter: b.1735 - d.1816; Peter left Ireland, 1765, to Ashgrove, Camden, NY, then Addington County, Ont. (Switzerville)
5) Margaret: (1) b.1738 - buried 29 April 1743
6) Margaret: (2) baptized 16 May 1743 - d.1807 in Augusta Twp, Ont. Margaret married (1) Philip Embury, on 31 Oct. 1758 (2) John Lawrence.
7) Christina: baptized. 27 Oct 1747- buried. 28 August 1750.
8) Catherine: b. 1749 - buried 13 Nov. 1755.

The Methodist Church, right on the commons in the center of the village, was built after John Wesley, a well known Methodist preacher who travelled around the country to share his views, came to the area urging the Palatines to return to the faithful habits of their forefathers.

It seems that they had been forgetting their beliefs and Wesley made several trips urging them to return to the more staid, church-going habits of their forefathers. After his third visit to the area he was delighted that they had returned to the fold. The church building was constructed with the help of Philip Embury in 1758. Embury lodged with the Switzers, who lived beside the commons during that time of construction, and on October 31 1758 he married Christopher's daughter Margaret. Philip and Margaret later crossed the ocean and helped start the Methodist Church in North America. Their contribution to the Methodist Church was recognized in 2005 when they were celebrated in the Bellville, Ontario, area.

We can see by the dates of subsequent births that some of Christopher and Catherine's children headed to North America as young people looking for new challenges. Their son, Martin, referred to as Martin Ye Younger in order to differentiate him from Martin Ye Elder born 1712 to parents John Michael and Mary Elizabeth, stayed in Rathkeale, Ireland and married Ann Barbara Legier on April 3, 1744. Ann Barbara was buried 15 May 1763. Their son Jacob is the son who will take us to the next generation.

<u>Martin and Ann Barbara's Children</u>

1) Catherine: baptized. 6 Jan. 1745, m. 17 Jan 1764 to **Garrett Miller**
2) Peter: baptized 25 Jan. 1747, m. 9 June 1772 **Catherine Tesky**. It is interesting that our present Canadian Prime Minister Harper's wife, Laureen, is a Tesky quite likely from this line, although there were several Tesky/Switzer marriages. OneTesky married another Jacob Switzer.

3) Christopher: baptized. 12 March 1749 - buried 4 July 1750, age 1 year
4) Mary: baptized. 8 Sept 1751, m. **John Shire** 3 May, 1785
5) Elizabeth: baptized 19 June 1754 - buried 8 Nov. 1755, age 1 year
6) Jacob: baptized 29 July 1756 at Pallas, City of Limerick
It is thought that he could be the man of that name from Pallas. (Jacob of Martin Ye Elder baptized 5 June 1756)
7) Barbara: baptized. 15 Jan. 1759, m. 29 Dec. 1778 to **John Long Martin. His** second marriage was to **Catherine Kennedy** (b 1732**)** on 12 May 1788, in Court Matrix

Martin and Catherine Kennedy's children:
1) Martin: baptized. 1 March 1789
2) Benjamin: baptized. 27 March 1791

It is important to mention here that the birth of *two* Jacobs**,** one born on **5th June 1756, son of Martin Ye Elder** and the other born **29 July 1756, son of Martin Ye Younger**, has created some confusion for those trying to follow our line. In order not to muddy the waters, this account does not include the genealogical data for Martin Ye Elder. Suffice it to say that both of these men are our possible forefathers, and for the sake of expediency, our family has taken the stand that Jacob, son of Martin and Barbara is our forefather**.** *"Until a treasured old Bible, or some other authentic resource surfaces, this is the route we will take"*. **(Comments made for a Switzer web site by Grant Ruske, family researcher from Edmonton who is married to one of our Benjamin's grandchildren).**

Records tell us that our **Jacob Switzer**, born at Castle Matrix, County Limerick was baptized in the Church of Ireland on 29 July 1756. It is believed that he was married to **Mary Ruckle,** who was one of the daughter's of Daniel of Ballingrane, County Limerick. She was born circa 1780 and it is felt that they were married in Ireland (not proven). So here we see another likely marriage between members of the Switzer/Ruckle families.

The Switzer and Ruckle families were connected several times over the years and were involved enough to hold joint picnics in Springbank Park, London, Ontario, on a regular basis. In fact, J Holmes, in an article entitled *Historical Sketch,* written for the 1925 Ruckle-Switzer Picnic, says that the one survivor of these two families, a Mrs. John Switzer, nee Ruckle, was able to verify that her Grandfather Jacob Switzer 1756 was a second cousin of her father, Daniel Ruckle. We do see that the name 'Daniel' appears in succeeding Switzer generations as is this family's custom of acknowledging forefathers.

We do not have all the details of this next generation. It is said that Jacob was the father of ten boys. During this time there was much passage between Ireland and Canada, and no doubt a great deal of work was required on arrival to begin the task of becoming successful settlers. Quite likely the pressing activities in this new land took precedence over recording accurate documentation of a growing family. We will continue to search for more information about their activities.

Children of Jacob and Mary Ruckle

1) William: b. 1805, m. Lavina Willis

2) Benjamin: b. 1809, Ireland - d. June 1885, Hanover, Ontario.

Sons John, Joseph, Reuben, Harvey J, Thomas, Bartholomew, Daniel, and **Christopher** were also attributed to this family. No additional data.

So many of the Palatine families married siblings, cousins, etc., that the details are rather foggy from this perspective. We will see in later chapters that this same situation arose here in Canada where large families who lived in the same vicinity often married brothers, sisters or cousins of neighbouring families. I remember as a young girl trying to sort out the web of cousins and aunts and their relationships in the Belfry/Taylor/Ney connection until it began to look like the "I'm my own Grandpa" syndrome. It seems that this family was enmeshed in similar situations.

Before we move on to the next stage of this family it is important to discuss some of the difficulties discovered in researching families in Ireland. Unfortunately a major stumbling block to accuracy resulted when much of the information about the Palatines was lost in a fire in 1922 that ruined the Archives in Dublin.

To further complicate the situation, the church registers from Rathkeale in County Limerick covering many records of the Palatine town lands survive only from 1742 ***(Henry J Jones).*** These were critical years of growth for many families so one must only offer an opinion about what happened, who married whom, and where they lived using whatever sources can be found.

It seems that Henry Jones's comment in his definitive recounting of these families is apropos as he asks readers to note his frequent use of *'perhaps, possibly* and *probably'*. Lacking official copies of the missing data, we really are only guessing.

Further to this situation, some hand written notations and anecdotes found among family sources tell us that some of our relatives might have lived in Tipperary.

Certainly this is an area closely bordering that of the Palatine holdings. As families grew it became difficult to continue subdividing their farms so secondary settlements were created. It was also true that much higher rentals were forcing people to find new home sites. It is logical then to see a move to nearby counties. Five Palatine families did obtain a lease from Sir William Barker of Kilcooly Parish dated 20 Oct 1773 for 186 acres in the Townland of Newpark, Co. Tipperary.

The names of those families were John Smeltzer, Daniel Ruckle, Baker and Lawrence, and John Switzer, with Leonard Shouldice, Jacob Shouldice and Paul Sparling joining in 1776 ***(W.G.Neely: Kilcooley: Land and People in Tipperary,1983***). We also learn that a John Switzer built a substantial two-story house on land that had been granted by Sir William Barker of Kilcooly Abbey to Protestant settlers. Possibly this is where one of the Switzer/Ruckle connections was made.

Often one query has led to another person with information, and then another. Each saga, recounted with generosity and enthusiasm, suggests that the drama of this family has captured much interest, even among folk who are not necessarily related. It is exciting to hear the versions and variations, and attempt to establish what really did happen lo those many years ago.

Much of my recounting of the Switzer background and early history is taken from *The Irish Palatine Family,* written by W.B. Switzer, revised 1993. I am indebted to William Switzer from Stratford, Ontario for lending me his copy.

When I was beginning my search of Switzer data, my husband and I were preparing for a cruise to South America and the Antarctic. One day the names of people with whom we would be cruising arrived at our door, and to my surprise a William and Lorna Switzer from Stratford, Ontario, were listed. Aha, I thought. Could we be connected? I resolved to try to meet for a chat during our holiday.

On arrival in Santiago, Chile, our tour company gave us a name card to hang around our necks so we could recognize our travelmates and learn each other's names. Embarkation required that we wind our way through orderly lines prior to boarding, and to my surprise there was William Switzer in another row. I called to him, and said that I would really like to talk to him and would try to connect later. The lines of course moved on.

Our next meeting was when we arrived at our assigned table that first evening, and found William (Bill) and his wife Lorna there among our other dining companions. Was fate involved? I certainly think so!

Bill and Lorna Switzer aboard the MS Amsterdam as we circled South America in January 2004

What a delightful group with which to share food and friendship for our three and a half weeks aboard. Bill and Lorna had travelled before with our four other tablemates so were already fast friends. They took us into their friendly circle, and we really enjoyed being part of their group.

Naturally our Switzer background and possible connection was a hot topic more than once.

It is most likely that we share relatives. Bill's forefathers were from our Jacob's older bother Michael's line so it would seem that we are related.

Switzers in Canada

Several researchers say that Jacob settled in Albion Township, Ontario, in 1832 with sons William, Harvey, Thomas, John S., and Daniel. Both B. Wesley Switzer and Harvey A. Switzer also list Benjamin, 1809, Joseph, Reuben, Bartholomew, and Christopher as being both brothers and sons of Jacob, as does Mary Wallace, another Switzer researcher with whom I have connected on the Internet, so we are assuming that this is correct. Documentation has not yet been available.

What we are certain of is that **Benjamin** (1809 - 3 June 1885) married **Mary Leonard** (1817 - 27 March 1879) in 1833 in Ireland. At that time his age was listed as 24 and her age was 16. As yet the date and location of their arrival in Canada is unclear so we are left with this mystery. It seems that it is highly likely that he did come to Albion with William and other brothers.

Benjamin put down roots on a farm near Newmarket in the West Gwillimbury area of Ontario, after first working as a coach driver for a family in Toronto, or Muddy York as it was then called. It certainly must have seemed logical to relocate where friends and kinfolk were already established. Other Palatine families had also discovered the delights of that part of Southern Ontario, known at the time as West and East Gwillimbury, and its popularity continued to grow. In fact, this rich area was a mecca for settlers from numerous places.

William Switzer, likely an older brother, had settled near by in 1832 with other Irish families, some named Beard and Shire who were from the Limerick area, too. William and the Shires had arrived on July 1, 1832 at Price's Corners, and were noted as the first settlers in that part of Medonte. These are some of the families who helped to settle southern Ontario.

William Switzer later became a well-known figure in local political circles, taking an active part in important decision making for the development of the Plank Rd. (the forerunner of Yonge St.), and the eventual settlement of the area. Benjamin, too, is listed as a councilor during the planning of the Plank Rd. *The Streetsville Review* recounted details of a meeting held in Jan 1840, which was called to discuss the continuing of the Plank Road from its terminus at the Townland to Norval, Georgetown and Guelph at which Benjamin Switzer seconded a motion during the business meeting. This adds weight to the assumption that William and Benjamin could have been brothers.

The most unusual names, East and West Gwillimbury, were created by John Graves Sincoe by using the first two syllables of his wife's maiden name, Gwillim. In the 1790s John Graves Simcoe was looking for an overland route from York (now Toronto) to Lake Huron, and this location was on the way. Some of the earliest settlers here were United Empire Loyalists and Quakers who no longer felt welcome in the United States, so this route was a natural entry point. Many settlers streamed up that artery from the Americas and the British Isles looking for places to homestead where political and religious freedom was both a right and a privilege.

As many of us know now, Yonge Street, as this throughway is now called, has played a significant role in the history of Ontario in the past, and even today it is one of the most widely used highways in the province of Ontario.

It now leads to 'cottage country' and to the great expanses to the North, but also allows commuters from outlying 'bedroom communities' quick access to Toronto. Well, perhaps *quick access* in not quite correct. Those busy daily lines of traffic tend to be anything but speedy quite regularly.

Today's commuters frequently bemoan the heavy traffic of this avenue to the north but it was a valuable asset in the development of the province.

Our great-grandparents Benjamin and Mary Leonard became the parents of eleven children; our grandfather Benjamin, the first son and eighth child was born in West Gwillimbury on 24 May 1848. He was baptized on 21 December in King Township.

<u>Children of Benjamin and Mary Leonard:</u>

1) Rachel: b.15 October 1834, m. **Charles Cuyler**

2) Elizabeth: b. 31 August 1836, m. **Mr. Campbell**,

3) **Rebecca: b.** 8 July 1838, m. **Mr. Touchbourne**
4) **Margaret**: b.12 May 1840 m. **Mr. Alward**,
5) **Alfred**: b. 1841 (died 1848 at age six),
6) **Lydia**: b. 30 August 1843, m. **Rev. James Clark**
7) **Mary:** b. 22 June 1845, m. **George Crozier/Krozier**
8) **Benjamin Jacob:** b. 24 May 1848, m **Caroline Amelia Kerr**, 13 Mar 1877, Methodist Parsonage, Hanover, Ont.,
9) **Daniel:** b.1850, m. **Mary Armstrong**
10) **Alfred:** b 1852, NM
11) **Joseph**: b.1855. NM

The Queen's Bush

An Order of Government was passed in April 1819 stating that Crown land was available to people willing to homestead in various areas of Ontario. The stipulation was that settlers would receive 200 acres if they started settling within a month of receiving a certification of location. They were required to eventually build a dwelling house and clear ten acres to the road as well as assume responsibility for half of the road in front of the clearing.

Despite these rather rigorous stipulations, many took advantage of this plan. It was rough work but was responsible for opening up southern Ontario to the many eager applicants flooding in from distant lands.

One of the sections being settled was known as the Durham Road, which, when surveyed in 1848-49, crossed the Owen Sound Road at the village of Durham. This road opened in sections between the years 1849-51, and 50-acre lots were being allocated along its course beginning in 1841. This area was known as The Queen's Bush and by 1850 settlement was well advanced along the route.

That year Benjamin and Mary and their family decided that they, too, would seek their fortune in what is called Bentinck Township and they settled on 17 Concession 1, North Durham Road, in Grey County. The land became theirs by crown grant deeded 1 December 1851.

One can imagine the anxious thoughts as they traveled through the rough, heavily forested terrain. Not only did they carry all of their provisions and implements but young baby Benjamin was carried, too. Part of their journey was via the Saugeen River and must have been somewhat less arduous than tramping through dense woods. Perhaps that is why their site was established along the Saugeen River's banks.

A log cabin and stable were quickly built. Family lore suggests that this particular site was chosen because it was the only suitable spot on the riverbanks for several miles in either direction. In fact, it was so close to the river that later young Benjamin could catch fresh fish for the family's breakfast by casting a line from the porch. No doubt the swirling river flowing by supplied many a tasty meals for the children who were born to these pioneers.

Written accounts of the challenges the settlers faced establish that life certainly wasn't a picnic. Many trees needed to be felled. Following that, it took about seven years for those huge tree stumps to disintegrate enough to be removed.

In the interim, the small kitchen garden, sorely needed to feed their ever-enlarging families, was eked from the land wherever the farmer's wife could find space. Snake rail fences made from rough logs guarded the plots from animals, and root vegetables blossomed. This is where our Great-Grandfather Benjamin grew and flourished.

Grey Township historical notes tell us that by the mid 1850s settlers were becoming more frequent. It also says some German families began arriving in the early 1850s. Their well chosen locations had good clay soil and their industriousness made them very successful homesteaders. Could our Switzer relatives be some of the people to which this account was referring?

A nearby town plot was surveyed in 1855 and the following year a hamlet first known as Buck's Crossing and later called Adamstown was established. This in turn expanded into a village, was renamed Hanover, and remains as such to this day. By 1868 the thriving town contained grist, saw and carding mills and a foundry and a cabinet factory that became the Knechtel Furniture Company.

Benjamin Sr. was a barn farmer and by 1850 he had built his own barn, so well constructed that it stood for over 100 years. The original horse stable and granary were still in use in the 1980s. Benjamin also built two limekilns, and these kilns later supplied most of the lime used for constructing homes in the town of Hanover. Even in this, the early part of the 21st century, the streets in Hanover are still lined with sturdy stone homes built from the products of those same kilns.

In 1874 Benjamin built a six-room, two-story building of grout construction, which was a mixture of sand, lime and gravel poured into forms, a forerunner of what we know as concrete. This became the popular method for building houses at that time. The outside walls were then plastered smoothly, and corner blocks of a heavier plaster were added for contrast and texture. Over the years two more rooms were added and the original 50 acres were enlarged to 265 acres.

In 1881 Benjamin's wife, Mary, died after which he sold the farm to his son, our grandfather, Benjamin Jacob. A cousin, Harvey, told reporter Isabel Oehm of the *Hanover Post,* that following family tradition, the farm had always been purchased through the generations. Harvey was quoted as having said, "*No son ever received the property as a gift from his father.*"

In turn, when Benjamin Jacob was ready to retire, he sold it to his son William, Harvey's father, who was able to pay for it by 1929 despite the Depression years. Mrs. Taylor, the reporter who wrote about Benjamin Jacob Switzer, began a 1931 *Hanover Post* article about him with the following short verse, looking back to an earlier time in their community.

Eighty long, long years ago a wilderness was here,
And man put powder in his gun and went to hunt the deer.
But times have changed a lot since then, man now prefers by far,
To roll along the broad highway in his bright, new motor car."

In this new millennium, we can readily see how much that hard work to which she referred has contributed to the development of the present large, attractive community. Hanover has thrived on a very successful furniture manufacturing trade. Households all over the country are familiar with the names of quality furniture such as Sklar-Peppler, J.S. Knechtel, and Krug Bros., to name a few.

One of the first furniture purchases for our Canadian home was made in 1963 on our return from France. We had toured their Sklar-Peppler showrooms and were delighted at the quality of the furniture and the wide choice available. And what was that purchase? We chose a beautiful creamy Italian Provincial bedroom suite for our infant daughter, Heather.

Its low dressers were topped with open shelves for progressive use from toys and dollies to textbooks and literature as she became a student. They are now in Heather's home in England and happily hold their household treasures gleaned over the years.

Several years ago one could still see the Switzer homestead with a very old cemetery nestled in one corner of a field near the main road into Hanover. Was this cemetery just a convenient location on the road to town, or did the community gravitate to this spot to bury their loved ones because the handcrafted coffins were made here and ready? Great-Great-Grandfather Switzer regularly crafted the coffins needed by the community.

Benjamin, his young son, often held the lantern well into the night so the coffins could be finished by the time they were needed. The tombstones in this quiet place are now tipped and pitted, but the names of many of those early settlers can still be seen carved in stone, mute testimony to those lives lived so long ago. In 2004 the family property was turned into a golf course with greens on both sides of the Saugeen. Would our forefathers have looked on in horror or approval?

The tombstones watch over the family homestead

The Switzer homestead near Hanover

The Switzer Homestead

Those hardy men gone before us had no time to think of leisure activities such as golf. Their daily duties included clearing land, burning underbrush, and ploughing with a wooden beam. This prototype of modern ploughs had a cast iron plate bolted to the end and was pulled by oxen. Another important implement was the harrow, a V-shaped wooden frame with iron spikes, which facilitated manoeuvring through the numerous stumps. No relaxing golf game for them. Instead, they worked hard all day, and at night unwound by carving furniture for their growing family's comfort.

Was my rocking chair made during those first early years? Was it whittled and cajoled into smoothness by Great-Great-Grandfather Switzer after long days spent out in those fields where bush and determination fought for supremacy? I would love to know. Regardless, it conjures up priceless, memories, and very deep emotions about those other times and places.

Mrs. Taylor continued her Hanover Post newspaper account by telling how ten-year-old Benjamin, his young son saw three wild ducks on the river one day. How exciting! He climbed up on the table, reached his father's flintlock gun, a gun much taller than he was, and proceeded to bag two of the ducks for their dinner. We shudder now at the idea of a ten-year-old having access to a loaded gun. Survival called for different rules at that time.

The old log schoolhouse stood at a site about a mile east of Hanover, where several trails converged. This was called Campbell's Corners and for a time was known as Magwood's Corners. I, too, remember the corner, which is still referred to as Campbell's Corners these many years later.

The older boys would appear in school as if by magic when the harvest had been completed. How the teacher must have dreaded their appearance on those frosty, late fall mornings.

For these hulking lads it was 'play-time' and the teacher's patience was regularly tested by their shenanigans. What fun to knock the props from under the benches bordering the room causing desks, books, and ink to scatter, and sometimes even the scholars toppled unceremoniously onto the floor! Their teacher must have rued the changing season when they coincided so dramatically with those big boys and their appearance for "some book-learning".

And so the years passed.

On February 13, 1877, Benjamin J. Switzer, now a dashing young man of 29 years, took the belle of the community, Miss Caroline Amelia Kerr, by the hand, and they were married in the old Methodist Parsonage on the county line, with the Rev. Josiah Green officiating.

Benjamin and Caroline
During their marriage

Caroline was the daughter of Daniel Thomas Kerr, (b. 1828, Scotland) and Elizabeth Egerton (b. 4 Jan. 1835, Staffordshire, England). She had been born at Erin near Guelph in July 1858 and came to Alan Park in the district as a girl.

Their first six years were spent on a farm at Ashfield, and on 4 November of that first year they became excited parents. What a surprise -- they were the proud parents of twins.

Children of Benjamin and Caroline Kerr

1) Margaret Lavina: b. 4 Nov. 1877, Ashfield Twp, Ont. twin,
m. **Wilson Thomas Hillis**

2) Mary Elizabeth: b. 4 Nov 1877, Ashfield, twin of Margaret Lavina, m.1) **George Helwig,** 2) **Adrian Augustinus**

Mary Elizabeth married her first husband, George Helwig, and lived in Hanover with their children. After his death she married a wonderful Dutch man named Adrian Augustinus. She was our grandmother's twin and we loved her as an almost-grand-mother. Aunt Mary was petite, and very loving. She always served little cookies, sometimes apple butter or a tangy apple cider when we visited her in their lovely Hanover home. Uncle Adrian had a wonderful Dutch burr when he spoke and he was very special. Mary lovingly visited him over the years after Aunt Mary died and we all cared for him very much.

3) Louisa Carolyn: b. 25 May 1879 m. **James Curtis**

4) Benjamin Daniel: b. 22 Aug 1880
m. 1910 **Keturah (Torry) Johnstone**

Benjamin and Torry, with daughter Florence Nielsen and grand daughter Deena Nielsen (Hansen). I visited them in Revelstoke, BC in the early 50s.

5) William James: b.13 July 1882 m. **Clara Lavina Willis**, d 21 Nov. 1965 (William eventually became owner of the Switzer property).

6) Laura: b.14 July 1884 - d. 15 June 1899 (of diphtheria)

7) Emma Rebecca: b. 20 Oct. 1886, m. 28 Nov. 1906 **Charlie Metcalfe**, d. 20 Oct 1892 in Saskachewan.

Mary, the 'heroine' of our story used to comment on 'Aunt Emma's Skies' every time she saw a lovely sky because her beloved aunt always spoke of the wonderful skies in Saskachewan.

8) Harvey Alexander: b. 6 Aug. 1889 - d.17 July 1944, m 1) **Edith Amelia Lawrence**, 18 Mar. 1914, Edson, AB. 2) **Mable Saul Bezanson,** b. 1892 - d. 1983.

Uncle Harvey became a pharmacist in Edson, Alberta, and increased the numbers of Switzers substantially by having 14 children.

9) Alfred Secord: b. 20 Oct. 1892 - d.13 Aug. 1935, m**. Susan Adams** June 1920.

Secord went overseas with the 147th Greys in 1915, served in France, and was gassed and sent to hospital. He never fully recovered from the effects although he was able to continue employment. Death came after complications from a fall on the ice, and subsequent surgeries.

10) Edith Ruby: b. 26 Sept. 1895 m**. Howard Allen** 1920, d. Feb. 1974 in Owen Sound, Ont.

Aunt Edith was a vibrant, young-at-heart lady who was struck by a truck in Owen Sound when she was 78. She sustained serious injuries and after first being treated in the hospital there was rushed to Toronto for more surgery. Unfortunately she did not survive. Her husband, Howard Allen owned a large cleaning establishment in Owen Sound. They had one son, Ray Allen, who continued running the family business and who died of ALS. During his lifetime he was International President of Rotary and while in this tenure he was responsible for having the International Rotarians support 'Sleeping Children Around the World (SCAW)', a charitable association to supply blankets, bed kits and other requirements for children in need. Canadian Murray Dryden and his wife, who were the parents of Canadian hockey legend Ken Dryden, started this organization. This is an ongoing charity for which volunteers, assisted by Rotarians, supply all necessary manpower, train workers in other countries and volunteer to deliver the bed kits to the children in the different countries.

In 1883 Benjamin and Caroline moved to the Durham Road near Hanover to a farm known then as the Chrysler Farm. Their last five children were born here. This is the farmhouse that has remained in the family until the present.

The family of Benjamin Switzer and his wife Caroline Kerr

Margaret Lavina is second left in the back row and her twin sister Mary is third from the left in the middle row.

Our story now moves to those twin sisters, Margaret and Mary. From all reports they were an attractive pair of young women, so similar in looks that they occasionally played tricks on their family and friends. In fact, once they chose to try to fool their gentlemen friends, Wilson Hillis and George Helwig when they were on a double date. All was going swimmingly as they sailed away in the cutter, until one of their swains quietly attempted to cuddle.

The twins Mary and Margaret Hillis

A healthy slap called a halt to that particular show of endearment. The young men assured them that they had known that the girls had changed places all along, but no one else really knows for sure.

On 12 December 1900 wedding bells rang out for daughter Margaret, who was 23 years old, and her chosen husband, Wilson T Hillis, aged 20. Their witnesses were his brother Samuel J. Hillis and her twin sister, Mary E Switzer. Following their wedding they moved to the nearby Hillis homestead.

And this brings us back to the Hillis farm where our mother, Mary and her sisters grew up.

Margaret Lavina Switzer and Wilson Thomas Hillis, December 12, 1900

Now that the Hillis and the Switzer families are joined, we will return to the Hillis/Switzer family homestead, which was the place where our saga began. The years were busy, as we have heard, and all members thrived.

In 1924 Mary, the little girl in the rocking chair with whom this story started was ready to continue her learning but their little one-room school did not include high school. This created somewhat of a problem. She was eager and really wanted to keep learning, so the decision was made that she should pursue her schooling in town at Hanover High School. The motto of this school was '*Enter to learn. Go forth to serve*'. That motto became Mary's creed, and was one that she continued to follow for the rest of her life.

Benjamin and Caroline Switzer move into Hanover to this home where Mary lived with them during the week

During the school week she stayed with her Switzer grandparents, who had by this time become the owners of our *story chair*. They had retired, turned their farm home over to one of their sons and moved into this home in Hanover. Living with them forged a very strong bond between them that lasted all of their lives.

It was an exciting time for her because it broadened her world to include 'town folks'. The school was brand new so Mary was one of its first students. There were oh, so many people to befriend, and being naturally gregarious, make friends she did.

Often these young folks made their way to the Hillis farm on weekends so that their fun and high jinks could continue. One delightful poem written by her in May 1924 tells of playing Hide and Seek with her classmates and their teacher, Miss Gordon. Not many teachers today would hide in the straw with their students, but these teens loved it. It was a time of new studies, making new friends and lots of new activities on which she thrived. Mary was a keen observer of life, and liked to record her thoughts and dreams in her diary. Her diary of January 29, 1925 reports that the weather was 27 degrees below zero and new folks named Belfry moved in next door. Little did Mary know, but the fates were about to play a decisive role in her future.

High School presented Mary with a wonderful smorgasbord of literature, language and such fascinating information to think about. How she loved it all, especially the English classes, and soon she was on the Literary Society Executive.

She loved her new school friends, she loved cheerleading, playing hockey, and skating was lots of fun, too. She had many girlfriends and boyfriends, but she was also rather intrigued by a very handsome gentleman living next door with those new neighbours, Mr. and Mrs. Arnim Belfry. He was Mr. Belfry's brother, Norman, who boarded with them.

Mary used to watch him back his truck out in the morning as he prepared to go to work on the Hydro where he was helping to build hydro lines in Eugenia Valley. She really did try to stand behind the curtain so he couldn't see her, but to her horror one morning, he turned and waved to her before driving off. How embarrassing! She resolved to be much more careful.

Eventually they exchanged greetings but she continued to call him Mr. Belfry for quite some time. Her April 1st diary entry says, *"Mr. Belfry brought me home from school in his car. I like him real well."*

Soon there was a flurry of excitement next door because a new baby had been born to Emily and Arnim Belfry, a wee daughter to be called Gloria. Gloria's Aunt Lu was visiting and she, always with an eye to what excite-

ment was in the air, or even ready to cause some, had a great idea.

Would Mary like to take a drive in Norman's new car and go to the hospital to see the baby with them? What a thrilling idea! Yes, Grandma Switzer thought it would be quite fine. Mary did, too, so off she went on what was to be the first date with the man who would become her soulmate and deep love. Mary's diary of April 23rd says, *"Norman Belfry took me for a ride to Durham, then almost over to Chesley. We had a wonderful ride and a good time."* It was hard for her to call him Norman and not Mr. Belfry, as he was quite a bit older than she was.

As was her habit, she penned a poem to commemorate that day, the last verse ending:

At last we came to Hanover and I did heave a sigh.
To think that I was nearing home and had to say, "Good-bye!"
But home we did not go just then, we turned around and away again
Over the road we fairly flew, and first thing I knew he held my hand too.
He was very nice to me I'm sure, and I liked him as well as most I knew.
That night when he left, he said, "May I call for you again?"
I answered, "Yes, Mr. B. Please do."

Mary Hillis Authoress, April 1925

That handsome man named Norman Ambrose Belfry became more and more important to Mary. Their friendship developed and by the fall of 1925 when she went to Toronto to attend teacher training at Normal School, she knew that he had stolen her heart. Mary remembers the next few years of their courtship as beautiful. There must have been anxious moments for Mary in giving her heart to Norm. He was nine years older than she was and anxious to settle down. And she did so want to be a teacher.

Mary and Norman fall in love

Mary's many gentlemen friends from school days would have been quite delighted if she had paid them more attention, and she really was fond of them and their company. She saw them often at school and in the community, and knew they were interesting and interested. Truth to tell, it seems that Norman was just a little bit jealous of them, too. According to her diaries, he occasionally became a bit testy after she had been in an activity with them and some of her other school chums. It couldn't have been easy for Norman to wait patiently for this vibrant young woman whom he really wanted to marry.

Mary was active in her school year at Hanover High School. She loved English, especially poetry, and could still quote many of her favourites, even decades later.

Hanover High School Literary Executive, 1925
Mary Hillis is front left.

When Hanover High School was celebrating its 75th Anniversary in 1999, Cheryl Waugh, a reporter from the *Hanover Post,* interviewed Mary, who was one of the first students. Mary spoke of a special teacher named Miss Simee, and credited her with instilling the love of poetry in those she taught.

With that statement, Mary launched into Shakespeare's famous soliloquy, "Let me play the fool: with mirth and laughter let old wrinkles come …" and she continued without faltering till the end of the quote. We were awed at her memory and enthusiasm.

Mary was not so enthusiastic about Mathematics, but loved Botany and Zoology. In fact, when there were insufficient students to form a class in those subjects in her final year, she elected to teach them to herself. Because she loved all aspects of nature she spent hours learning the various species and all of the Latin names.

She sailed through all of the matriculation exams with ease although the ones she had taught to herself were the subjects with the most difficult exams that graduating year.

Normal School

When Mary attended Normal School in Toronto in 1925/26, she boarded with her Aunt Ella (Grant), her father's youngest sister. What a thrill to be in the city now, although leaving Norman behind was a wrench. They wrote regularly, and their affection for each other grew stronger. Aunt Ella and Uncle Wesley welcomed her to their home, and introduced her to their part of Toronto, to their friends and to their church. Mary loved being with them, and their affection for each other lasted for all of their lives.

Ella Hillis Grant and Wesley Grant, Mary's aunt and uncle, with whom she lived while at Normal School

Mary was a lovely girl and managed to turn heads with her cheery approach to life. There was a teacher called Mr. Black at the Normal School, who noticed. In fact, he took quite an interest in getting to know Mary. He took her to shows, for drives and to the theatre. He also was extremely helpful. He made it a point of helping her with useful pointers for practice teaching and helped her prepare for exams.

Mary did appreciate this. She also enjoyed having the opportunity to experience some of Toronto's activities with him. Big city life was exciting.

Ostensibly he was just trying to help her acclimatize to city life and help her prepare her lessons. But those surprise visits and long phone calls pointed to the fact that he was more interested than she realized. He often dropped in to Aunt Ella and Uncle Wesley Grant's home where she was staying, visiting with them, played card games and often took her to church. Such a friendly gentleman!

From this standpoint we appreciate that he was quite smitten with this naive young lady. But Mary was still unaware that he had any interest in her. She did love the delights of Toronto. She also loved roaming through big department stores like Eaton's and Simpson's with her girl friends, having treats of orangeade and chocolates, and dancing and playing card games, etc., with the many young men who were at school.

Life in the big city was wonderful, but she never neglected the daily letter to Norman, or he to her. His letters were thrilling and they shared their hopes for the future and their affection for each other. One has to wonder how Norman felt when he heard about the dances and outings she took, but he trusted her judgment and was willing to wait for her.

Lesson plans still had to be done and most of the time Mary sailed through with good criticisms. One lesson on 'ice harvesting' was not a success and she smarted under the criticism. I can imagine that she was flying pretty well on nerve on that one!

She loved Glee Club, Lit Society, in fact, everything. She also loved life and all of the new friends that she had made.

Later in April she finally had her eyes opened to the fact that Mr. Black was much too interested. The day he asked her to be his date at a faculty dance was quite a revelation to her. She was aghast. At last she understood that he was very interested in having a future with her. How dreadful! A very long, serious talk was in order. She quickly gave him to understand that she did not want to pursue this path, and that she was in love with Norm. Eventually Mr. Black, whom she did finally refer to by his first name in her diary, graciously bowed out, but he assured her he would not completely give up until she had set a date to marry. In fact, he wrote to her during the summer holidays and did send his good wishes on her marriage so had apparently been following her activities.

The summer of 1926 her graduation from Normal School became official when she received notification that she was finally a qualified teacher. Three cheers for Mary! What a thrill it was to see that certificate. Now the rest of her life should unfold as planned. But a teaching position would certainly help!

That was a very busy summer. Together with her mother and sisters, they picked hundreds of pails of berries, cherries and red currants,. Then these were either sold in town or preserved. Cows had to be milked, milk separated and butter churned as well. Morning and evening chores were a daily requirement on this farm, as was baking, so these activities were ongoing.

But one of Mary's most important functions during that time was sending a flurry of letters of application. How she wanted to put her teaching training into practice! As soon as her many applications had been posted her anxious watch began.

The daily mail deliveries were almost too hard to wait for, and frequently she paced the long lane to the mailbox with her heart in her mouth.

Mary's oldest sister, Florence, was already married by this time. She and her swain, John Emerson Hudson from a neighbouring farm family were married in 1922 and their first son John Wilson 'Jack was a born in 1925. The girls all loved his antics and I imagine they were delighted to take him for walks and enjoy his gurgles. Later two more boys, Jim and Gary, joined the Hudson family and they brought great joy to both households.

Florence Hillis and Emerson Hudson married in Hanover in 1922

The farm home of the Hillis family seemed to be a natural place for folks to gather. In a diary entry on August 15, Mary says that the cattle broke into the oats and they had some difficulties getting them sorted out. Then in the evening six carloads of friends dropped in, they made ice cream and had a great time. Most of us now would have a small fit if six carloads of friends decided to call on us unannounced.

Hopes were often raised about a teaching position, and then just as often dashed. Those 80 or so letters of application just seemed to evaporate into thin air subsequent to being posted. At long last she did receive a positive reply. A school was available at Berkley where the trustees offered her placement in their school for the yearly salary of $850.

The idea of over 40 pupils in Grades One to Eight didn't daunt her one bit. Youth was on her side and Mary quickly accepted. Her optimism was somewhat shaken, however, when she first saw her new school just before the end of the summer. It was small, not very modern, heated by woodstove, and quite a distance from her beloved home and her Norman.

Mary and Norm had reached an agreement several months earlier that they would eventually marry. At that time, young women schoolteachers could not be employed if they were married so she knew she could only plan for a short teaching career. Many of Mary's friends from Normal School also found to their chagrin that they were not eligible for a job if they married. It was a dreadful choice. Some chose to marry and keep their marriages secret. This often proved difficult if distances were involved or if a pregnancy ensued. Norman was older and ready to settle down, but he appreciated the fact that Mary had her heart set on being a teacher. He was proud of her and readily agreed that she should have an opportunity to practice the profession which she had worked so hard to attain.

And so she began her teaching career that September, proud, scared and very excited. Each day was a test of her energy and ingenuity as she tried to encourage students from Grade One to Eight to settle down, work hard and master all the required subjects. Not all days were successful and quite likely there were many tears of frustration in her room at night. For a while some of those hulking boys who were disinterested in school made life very difficult for her by getting up onto the school roof to romp at recess and lunchtime. She pulled herself up to her full height of four feet eleven and three quarter inches, used her most serious voice to scold them, and before too long she did get them on her side. Perhaps the detentions helped to convince them. She also doubled her efforts to make the material interesting and challenging, too.

Her pupils learned that Mary was not about to let them rule. She was decisive and disciplined -- a fact not missed by the chairman of the school board whose son she had to keep after class for his upsetting classroom behaviour. This prompted a rather speedy visit from the unhappy father.

Mary stood her ground and insisted that her decision was final and that punishment was required. We imagine that it wasn't easy to pull her tiny frame up to its maximum height and face this angry official, but she did and it worked. She had their complete confidence after that. In fact, after the New Year they gave her a small raise in pay.

She loved to regale us with the challenges, the shenanigans and successes of those early teaching days. The big boys liked to test her, but did learn that she was 'the boss'. And so she became a valuable, respected member of the community.

Of course the encyclopedia salesmen found these young teachers too. One can imagine the guilt trip if the teacher said she wasn't interested. But Mary was interested, and felt that it would be an important purchase, so became the proud owner of The World Books that first fall, a $70 dollar purchase. No doubt she spent hours devouring them, as we did later in our home.

It must have seemed like a great thing to have because in my own home we also made a purchase of the same series when our children became old enough to read.

This is how the enlarged school at Berkley looked in 1990

Mary's diary tells us that as school started in January 1927 she found that she was to have two new students to teach. She told her diary that they were quite a pair of dumbbells, but we are sure that she didn't let them know that is what she thought. The next week there were two more.

The small classroom was fairly groaning at the numbers. Likely Mary was too. Sometimes families waited until their children were six before they registered them. Often they lived a distance from their neighbours and so their children were good company. In all, she had 49 pupils that year. This must have been a tremendous amount of work for Mary, but she was keen and loved it all.

Living in the community and boarding with a local family had its interesting aspects. The family son was rather taken by such an attractive young lady, and watched her comings and goings quite carefully, maybe even too carefully. If Mary was at a 4H meeting with others and he disagreed with the lateness of the hour of her return, he would sometimes lock the gate, making it necessary for her to climb over in order to get to the house and to her bed. Getting over the gate was difficult, quite unladylike and very annoying. And once she even tore her dress in the process. She was vexed at him but still continued to attend the local activities.

She did, however, make it clear to everyone that she was committed and had already given her heart away so that there would be no misunderstanding. Almost daily letters from Norm and occasional weekend visits home sufficed to keep their love strong.

Those frequent letters between Mary and Norm were an important link for both of them. During that time a rather overzealous young lady in the post office grew a little too curious about their messages. The teacher and her 'doings' were cause for much conjecture. Finally this young lady's curiosity got the better of her and she decided to tamper a bit.

Mary was enraged when her letters were snooped, and faced the young woman with threat of dire consequences should it continue. It worked! From then on problems ceased and the love letters went on their merry way without delay.

One of the interesting aspects of living in the community was frequently being invited home with one or another of her students. The teacher was of much interest to the parents and they truly wanted to get to know her. When they asked her to come home with their children she would be treated to the best the family could offer, warm hospitality, and after dinner a bed for the night. Then off to school she and her pupils would go the next morning.

As one can imagine, if Jennie had the teacher this week, who would be the next lucky one she would visit? It kept Mary busy, but gave her invaluable insight into the lives of her students and how their family situations and learning patterns might impact on their success. Mary loved people so this particular part of her growing up was especially satisfying for her. Educators now know that learning can be enhanced or complicated by life's situations but we imagine that it was a rather novel approach in 1926. So Mary was quite innovative in her approach to teaching the whole child.

That year the dreaded visit from the Inspector came on May the 16th. Every new teacher shook at the thought of this event, and Mary was no exception. Thankfully, he told her that everything was neat and tidy and that she had excellent discipline. Whew! The work of being consistent had paid off.

Mary had been meeting members of the Belfry clan on short drives with Norm during that first year. Norm also taught her to drive his new Chevy coupe so it was an exciting time. Brother Roy and his wife Lu lived in nearby Durham and she already was friends with brother Arnim and Emily, Lu's sister, who lived next door to Grandma Switzer in Hanover. Norm's sister Laura and her husband Linus Vasey were within driving distance too. And during that busy summer of 1926 they also went to Victoria Harbour on Georgian Bay to meet Norm's parents, Sherman and Esther Belfry. It was a happy visit and the beginning a life-long, affectionate friendship.

When she returned home to Hanover over Christmas holidays in 1927, she was delighted to receive her lovely diamond from Norm when they picked him up at the train station on Dec. 27.

Her diary says,

"Dad took us to town in the sleigh to meet my dearest Norm at the CNR. He is the same wonderful fellow. He slipped my engagement ring on my finger with a wonderful kiss. Oh, dearest, may I be good for you, you wonderful man."

At the end of the school year of 1927/28 she handed in her resignation in order to prepare for her wedding. The school district did not want to lose this valuable teacher and Trustees really coaxed her to stay. However, her promise to Norman stood and she tearfully left the position that she loved so much. She was thrilled with the going away party that the families planned for her, and off she went with wonderful parting gifts and their many good wishes.

The farm was a hive of industry that summer.

Exciting plans were afoot. Her sister Beatrice was busily organizing for her own wedding to the love of her life, Oliver Harrison, so it was a busy time. Beatrice and Oliver were married at home and Mary and the other sisters made sure that all was perfect for the happy couple. The happy couple started married life in Mildmay, Ontario, a small town not far away, and they were to remain there for the rest of their lives. They were very involved in the community, and enjoyed raising a family of three boys, Earl, Ross and Alan, and also a daughter, Jean Marie, who was called Jean.

Oliver Harrison and Beatrice Hillis, June 14 1928

Mary Marguerite Hillis, Circa 1926 Toronto Normal School Graduate

The Belfrys

During their long courtship Norm told her about his large family, the antics of his brothers and sisters, and many stories about the coming of that first Belfry family to Canada. We have always been told that our Belfry family history really began on the high seas off the coast of Grand Banks, Newfoundland. What an unusual beginning.

I guess you could say, however, that this part of our saga really began in France. Our oral tradition and written accounts tell us two of the passengers on a ship bound for the New World were Peter Belfry or Pierre Balfée, born in Northern France and his wife, Catherine Lachioness Young (b. about 1755). Her name could also have been a rather garbled version of the French 'La Jeunesse' or the anglicized form YOUNGER, and she was described as the daughter of an English lady.

The fascinating story about Jacob, the first of their children and how he made his appearance just as land was being sighted has been part of our family lore for decades. This is the one who was to become our Great Great-Great-Grandfather. What an auspicious time to arrive on the scene just as this young couple was about to break ground as new settlers. Such a dramatic beginning! Jacob, whom we are told was born off the rocky land called the Grand Banks, has been heralded as the forefather of a tribe of Belfry's such as he could scarcely have imagined. The date was May 28, 1777.

But wait! Could there have been another scenario?

In searching the archives now stored in Montreal and Quebec City, some interesting alternatives have surfaced.

During my quest in Montreal, I met Jacques Gagné, a Quebec Genealogist, while we were both searching in the library of the Quebec Family History Association. Jacques, who is an authority on early French emigration, offered me his valuable expertise. He also shared some historical observations, and suggested some other possible scenarios.

For one, he told me that after 1759 and the Plains of Abraham loss to the English, emigration from France to Canada had been stopped. The exceptions to this were highly educated people such as doctors, educators, notaries, judges, nurses, or priests. Military personnel were included in this acceptable list. French farmers or peasants were no longer welcome, although there were no restrictions on settlers from the British Isles. Thus, Jacques wondered if our Jacob's parents could have been educators, which might have explained why he was later placed in the Seminary in Quebec City after his parents' early death.

It seemed that no records of our Jacob's birth could be found in Quebec City. However, Jacob could possibly have been baptized anywhere along the shores of the St. Lawrence where dozens of villages existed in 1777. There were many such places and there is no likelihood of tracking them down.

The suggestion was made that some of the alternate spellings of the name might be explored. As we know, names were often misspelled because they were not heard correctly, or written incorrectly because of language and/or interpretation. Add to this the personal handwriting styles of different scribes and we realize that conditions were ripe for the endless variation in the names of emigrants. Computers were not around to tidy up our careless script and/or keep multiple copies of data as we have come to expect today.

The Bellefeuille Possibility

This brings us to the name Bellefeuille (or Bellfée). As this name cropped up as a possibility clue to our history, I realized that the hand-written penciled name of 'Bellefeuille' was at the beginning of my photocopy of the Belfry family history. A question mark was beside it.

It is also the name that my first cousin Lee Bryen (Leona Belfry) had arrived at in her Belfry genealogical search a few years ago. In participating in online discussions regarding the Belfry forefathers, she found a number of people who felt there was merit in considering this avenue.

Certainly the names could sound alike, especially if the English pronunciation of Bellefeuille (Bellfée) was used. It is therefore quite possible that this could be the genesis of our tribe. With no trace of the name Belfry to be found until our Jacob surfaced in Ontario when he was about 20 years old, we will look at what the archives have to say about the Bellefeuille family. I include Lee's data, melding it with what I have so far gleaned from local archival accounts, and we will see where it takes us. Going from the known family information found in our printed Belfry book, Pierre was the father of our Jacob. Can Pierre be found in the records? Yes, he can if he is called Pierre Bellefeuille! So that is where we will start this alternative story.

Although this has not been authenticated it is an interesting possibility. As well, it gives us an idea of how the emigration from France fits into the Canadian cultural mosaic.

<u>Bellefeuille Genealogy Data</u>

Going back several generations before Jacob takes us to Rene Bellefeuille and his descendants: New websites have become available, showing French emigration to North America. We are told that **Rene Bellefeuille** was a cabinet maker/innkeeper and married **Madeleine Gendre** in Deux-Sevres on 8 Feb. 1695.

1. Rene Bellefeuille was baptized at Eglise paroisse Saint-Martin, Pioussay, France. b. about 1688 – d.12 Mar. 1758, in Quebec. Historical documentation says that Rene was an innkeeper and he and his wife, Madeleine Gendre, arrived in Canada 2 July 1695.

Their son was

2. Louis Bellefeuille, b. about 1691 in Pioussay, France, m. **Marie Josephe Auvray**, on 20 Mar. 1735 (daughter of Jacques Auvray and Marie Mezeray), who was b.1706, Quebec and d. 14 May 1758, Quebec. It is interesting that Rene and his son Louis died within a couple of months of each other, possible as a result of rampant disease.

The first recorded reference to Louis in Quebec documentation is from 1719. His occupation was listed as a soldier in the navy and in Gannes Company. His place of birth was listed as Pioussay (St. Martin) Two-Sevres. This could well be our forefather.

Children of Louis Bellefeuille and Marie Auvray

1) Marie Josephe Bellefeuille: b. about 1732

2) Thomas Louis Bellefeuille: b. 8 Dec. 1735

3) Marie Louise Bellefeuille: b. 21 April 1737, Quebec.

1) m. **Francois Edine Laviolette:**11 Nov. 1754, Quebec (son of Michel Edine and Anne Bon). d. before 1760, Quebec.

(2) m**. Joseph Berdin Lafontaine:** b. about 1721 - m. 18 Nov. 1760, Quebec, (son of Denis Lafontaine and Marie Savard,) d. 11 June 1784, Quebec.

4) Francois Stanislaus Bellefeuille: b.16 Oct. 1738, Quebec, d. 4 Feb. 1781 (age 73)

m. **Marguerite Anne Rancourt:** b. 1718 - d. 6 Jan. 1784, m. 7 July 1761, Quebec (age 23)

4) Marie Monique Bellefeuille: b. 25 Mar. 1741, Quebec - d.11 Feb. 1793 (age 53)

****5).Pierre Bellefeuille**, b.15 May 1741, Quebec - d. 6 Aug 1787, Montreal, m. **Marie Antoine Louise** Bellefeuille, b. 22 Dec. 1747, Quebec, - d. 16 Feb. 1782 Montreal (age 35)

Daughter Marie Louise

Child of Marie Bellefeuille and Francois Laviolette

****Marie Louise Laviolette:** (Daughter of Marie Louise and Francoise Laviolette),
b. about 1757 - d. before 1784, m. **Pierre Voyer Lejardinier**, 24 Nov. 1777, Montreal

****3. Pierre Bellefeuille:** (son of Louis and Marie Auvray) b. 15 May 1741, Quebec - d. 6 Aug. 1787, Montreal, (age 46). He is likely our forefather.
m. **Marie Josephte Pigeau Lajeuness:** 21 Jan. 1765, Montreal, d/o Rene Pigeau and Marie Rouleau. b. 15 Jan. 1742/43, Montreal - d.16 Feb. 1782, Montreal (age 39)

Children of Pierre Bellefeuille and Marie Lajeunesse

1) **Pierre Belleufeille:** b. 24 Oct. 1765, Montreal. Said to have had two sons
2) **Male Bellefeuille:** b. 5 Jan. 1768, Montreal - d. 5 Jan. 1768 (at birth)
3) **Marie Marguerite Bellefeuille**, b. 15 Aug. 1769, Montreal,- d. 22 Dec. 1769 (age 4 months)
4) **Laurent Bellefeuille**, b. 24 Oct. 1771, Montreal - d. 24 July 1799, Montreal
5) **Jean Baptiste Bellefeuille**, b. 22 Jan. 1774, Montreal - d. abt 1783, m. **Victoire Hunault-Deschamp**, 31 Jan. 1803, Repentigny, Quebec.

*6) **Jacques Bellefeuille**, b. 29 May 1776 Montreal

This Jacob Belfry's birthdate coincides with our Jacob's May 28, 1777 date with only slight variations and is our most likely ancestor.

Marie, whose dates are as follows, could be the daughter our Belfry book mentions who married someone in Montreal

4) Marie Antoine Louise Bellefeuille: Louis, Rene, b. 22 Dec. 1747, Quebec - d. 8 Mar. 1786, Montreal (age 39), m. **Francois Bardet Lapierre** 6 Feb 1769, Montreal

Their child

1) **Marie Louise Bardet Lapierre**, b. about 1770. m. **Joseph Prudhomme,** 9 Sept 1793, Montreal.

Our Forefathers

So, let us consider how this information impacts upon what we have always felt was correct. There certainly is a strong similarity in the names of Pierre Bellefeuille (Pierre Belfry) and Marie Lajeunesse (Catherine

Lajeuness) who had a son Jacques Bellefeuille (Jacob Belfry). The dates of the deaths of Pierre 1787 and Marie (Catherine) 1782 also correspond to the dates we have all read in the Belfry book. That brings us to Jacques/Jacob? We do know that he was on the run from the Seminary and it is quite possible that he changed his name to a more Anglo Saxon one in order to distract those who were looking for him. Quite possibly he also gave himself a rather romantic birth story which would be difficult to authenticate.

Cousin Lee's search says that Louis came as a soldier, a need that was common at that time. There are many records of soldiers and naval personnel who came to Canada in those years to help shore up the defenses against the English.

Many ports in the north of France had regular trips to Canada to bring soldiers, adventurers and much needed professional and educationalists. Her research told her that Louis had a drinking establishment in Quebec City. Pierre, his son, was a saddle maker and one of Joseph/Jacob's brothers was a soldier. It was also discovered that one family of Bellefeuille's from Trois Rivieres definitely changed their name to Belfry and later settled in Michigan. Thus far, no Belfry genealogists that we have heard about have found any trace of Jacob Belfry in Quebec.

An archivist in Quebec City recently carried out a search in both the general files of Seminary of Quebec for me, as well as in the students' files. He looked for Belfry, Balafee and Bellefeuille and found no trace of any one who could be a match for our elusive Jacob. It is therefore likely that some or all of the original history is incorrect. We must remember that Jacob was only about seven years old when he was left an orphan, and we can assume that he was not especially familiar with the details of his family's background. He did have a classical education so could have been in the Seminary under another name. The Belfry historian, Peter DeGuerre has said that much of his information was gleaned from Oran Belfry who was then in his eighties. Given memory and the time laps, errors could well have occurred.

What we do know is that Jacob was a resourceful fellow, and will thus continue with the story of Jacob, our patriarch.

Few details of their first few years in Canada remain. Hardly surprising! We shudder at the problems they must have faced building a home, having several children and surviving in this very young country. We do know other children were born to this couple. One son was called Peter (Pierre) and another became a surveyor, went to Maine, and no information has been found about his life. Some accounts tell us that

Peter had two sons who became Roman Catholic priests, and a daughter was apparently married to a M. Lafontaine in Montreal. This could be Marie who married M. Lapierre. Hopefully we can find more on this line although both names Lafontaine and Lapierre are very common French Canadian family names, and it would be well nigh impossible to trace them without parents' names or birthdates.

Our book source says that Catherine died during those first years, and her husband, Peter, died in about 1784 in Quebec City when Jacob was seven years old. According to his will, Peter directed his friend to place the children in the Roman Catholic College or Seminary in Quebec City to be educated for the priesthood. This very well established Catholic school gave a classic education as well as trained students for the priesthood.

The following description of the college is from *The Belfry Family*, by Peter DeGuerre, which was written in 1888:

The Seminary

"The college or seminary of education was founded and endowed many years ago by the French Government. It is situated in the heart of the Upper Town, in a pleasant and commanding situation, overlooking the place of the Falls of Montmorency. The centre building of the college is one hundred and eighty feet long and four or five stories high and there are two wings of proportionate dimensions. The massive walls are of stone, of substantial workmanship. There is a chapel attached, also spacious gardens and offices. Its system of education has become liberal. Those who desire instruction in theology, receive it, and those who don't are under no obligation to adhere to the doctrines of the Church of Rome. It has professors who teach arithmetic, history, geography, the sciences, philosophy, mathematics, and the Greek Latin, French and English languages."

The details of Jacob's life recounted here and the information on his large family have been paraphrased from Peter DeGuerre's book entitled *The Belfry Family*, published in Toronto in March 1888.

In the preface to Mr. DeGuerre (1824 - 1906)'s work he says:

"The Belfry Family was more than an ordinary family; it is an uncommon occurrence to find a family so large, having the same longevity. Sixteen children that grew up to be men and women is not known to the writer in the County of York, and it is a possible question whether a parallel can be mentioned or is in existence in the Province of Ontario."

Certainly we know from this prospective that infant mortality, difficulties of pioneer life, illness, harsh climate and geographical conditions all took a serious toll on the early settlers. No doubt this family felt the ramifications of these conditions as well. We do, however, celebrate that they were able to live happy, successful lives and produce many, many heirs.

Storyteller DeGuerre went to school in Queensville, Ontario, with four of the younger Belfry brothers, descendants of Jacob. Later he married their younger sister Clarissa (Clara). DeGuerre knew the family well so agreed to chronicle the family history when Mr. Belfry's grandchildren made the request following a family picnic. This congenial family regularly got together for large annual picnics or winter gatherings. Stories of escapades were a regular part of their socializing. So DeGuerre, as a well-informed friend and in-law, was in a good position to be their scribe.

Mr. DeGuerre bemoaned the fact that he had no historical training. But because of his close association with these in-laws, he agreed to compile their history from anecdotes, memories of, and conversations with various sources. His preface says that he has tried to condense his information so that his work would be available at a moderate price. One wonders what that price might have been in March of 1888.

Because of him we have vivid descriptions of the life and times of these early settlers who made a committed contribution to the County of York and to Canada as it is now.

But that was only the beginning! See how far we've come, and just imagine where we and our heirs have yet to go. The roots have grown deep and the branches have stretched far and wide.

Mr. DeGuerre's detailed information was written quite descriptively. He describes the physical and emotional characteristics of this cast of thousands rather completely. We were able to borrow a copy of this book in the 1950s and I remember reading it aloud to my Grandmother (Ney) Belfry. At the time I was a young, thin teenager and I was aghast to read about women five foot one weighing 160 pounds being described as comely and most attractive. Laughingly I commented that they must have been carrying huge bags of flour. In retrospect, and with the added girth and understanding of 'maturity', I imagine they were much like those of us whom we see every day.

This account simply tries to retell the facts as having been recorded by DeGuerre, with the addition of a few anecdotes so that readers can glimpse the lives and times in which they lived.

Jacob Belfry Grows Up

From the age of seven, Jacob lived at the Seminary in Quebec City where he was required to rise at five to attend mass. This early hour did not seem to bother him, and he continued to be an early riser throughout his life.

Ten productive years were spent in this institution. However, there were some specific aspects of college life that he did not find quite as acceptable as rising at dawn.

He did not care for the food, nor did he get enough to eat. He also was forming his own opinions, some of which did not quite reflect the opinions of those in charge. He thought it quite improper that priests could pardon the sin of other humans, and the fact that priests could not marry was very much against his inclinations.

Finally teen-aged, strong-willed and independent, Jacob, decided to take matters into his own hands and left the college without permission or discharge. His guardians followed him, and not only did they bring him back, they also bound him to learn the cooper trade as a punishment. Presumably this meant that his studies toward the priesthood were put aside, so at least one of his hopes was realized. The trade as a cooper was later to become very important, as most produce grown, produced or acquired was stored in barrels of all size. Consequently a ready supply was constantly needed. Storage vessels were in great demand to transport all manner of goods along the rivers and byways of Canada and Jacob's expertise proved to be a decided asset.

Some years later he left the seminary without permission again, leading to some interesting developments. At 20 years of age while absent without permission, he met a college mate who tried to entrap him into serving in the British army. At that time an attractive payment was made for leads to new recruits. No doubt his old classmate was interested in this payment so Jacob was left bound to a chair in an inn to await capture. The 'friend' expected him to be caught and thrown into the army, but Jacob was a strong young man and managed to get free with some assistance from others. From there he travelled west to Brockville, Ontario, where he decided to settle.

Jacob and Joanna

One day when walking on a street in town, Jacob met a comely young woman named Joanna Sherman. He was captivated! It seems that the feeling was mutual and eventually the two were married in 1797 when Jacob was 22 years old and Joanna was 16.

Joanna, the attractive 16 year old who caught Jacob's eye on the streets of Brockville, came with a rather interesting background of British forefathers, some of whom either came to America on the Mayflower, or settled in the Plymouth/New England around the same time as those eager Plymouth Puritans. We will pause here to see where her family roots developed.

Her family name was Sherman (at first spelled Shearman) and originally they came from Germany. Our available records date only from their early lives in England. The name Sherman will continue to appear in the Belfry line, but always as a given name rather than as a family one. We will see that their heirs will frequently use the name Joanna or Joanne as well. In tracking Joanna's family history we will start with her mother's family.

<u>Joanna's Maternal Family</u>

1st Generation**: Nicolas Snow:**: b. 1530, Eng. - d. about 1622, Hoxton, Eng.
m. Elizabeth Harwoode, b.1535, Stepney, Eng.

2nd Generation: Son **Nicholas Snow:** b. about 1578, Hoxton, Middlesex, Eng, - d. Eng 1605/1669
m. Mary Walker, b.1580, m. 5 May 1599, Stepney, Eng. (b. 1580 Stepney, Eng.)

3rd Generation: Son **Nicholas Snow:** b. 25 Jan. 1599/00, Hoxton, Eng. - d. 15 Nov 1676, Eastham, Barnstable, Mass., m. Constance Hopkins 22 May 1627. b.1606 - d.??

4th Generation: Son **Mark Snow:** b. 9 May 1628, Plymouth, Mass. - 9 Jan. 1694/95, Barnstable, Mass.
m. Jane Prince, 1 Nov. 1637 - ??, b. ? d. 1659/60.

5th Generation: Son **Nicholas Snow**: b. 6 Dec. 1663, Barnstable, Mass. - d. about 1754, Rochester, Massachusetts, m. Lydia Shaw (b 1672, Eastham, Barnstable, Mass.) on 4 April 1689.

6th Generation: Son **Prince/Prence:** (26 Dec. 1707 - d. before 22 Feb. 1758) m. Mary Sturtevant, 3 Nov. 1708 - d ?? Plymouth, Mass.

7th Generation: Daughter **Mary Snow:** 30 Oct. 1729 d.1752/5, Ware, Mass m. 20 April 1749 **to Prince Sherman** 26 Feb. 1753 – 1798.

8th Generation: Daughter **Joanna Sherman:** (26 July 1781 in Ware, Hampshire - 25 Aug. 1847), Queensville, York.

As seen here, children of succeeding generations were frequently given the name of their father as happened in the Switzer family and indeed in most families. This custom continues to thwart the progress of future genealogists.

Joanna Sherman's Paternal Forefathers

1.) **William Sherman:** b.?? - 25 Oct. 1679, m. Prudence Hill on 23 Jan. 1639.
2.) Son **John Sherman:** (23 Feb. 1646 - 5 Nov. 1722), m. Jane P Hatch, nine children among them
3.) Son **John Sherman:** (17 Oct 1682 - 29 Sept 1765), m. Sarah Baker on 26 March 1711/12. Had nine children, among them,
4.) Son **Samuel Sherman:** (b. 13 Jan. 1724 - 29 Jan. 1811) Ware, Mass., m. Mary Snow on 20 April 1749 (30 Oct, 1729 - 1752/1755). Among their children was
5.) Son **Prince Sherman:** (26 Feb 1753 - between 1792/9), Ware, m. Mary Submit Rogers on 27 Jan 1776, (b. about 1759 in Brockville, - d. 1804) Phillipsville, Leeds Co., Ont. Among their children was
6.) Daughter **Joanna Sherman: 26 July 1781 in Ware, Hampshire - 25 Aug. 1847, Queensville, York

Sixteen children were born from the union of Joanna and our Jacob Belfry, and we will take a look at their lives, and at many of their offspring along the way. Their story shows their pioneering spirit and courage in settling a new land.

Joanna, the daughter of Prince Sherman and Mary Submit Rodgers had been born at or near Ware, Massachusetts, on July 26, 1781. With her family, she had left Massachusetts in 1787 for Vermont, and they journeyed from there to Canada around 1792. Later, a grandson of Prince Sherman, a William Sherman of Plum Hollow, wrote that,

"My grandfather was scarcely settled when he took sick and died, leaving his wife and family to care for themselves. Joanna was the eldest of a family of six children she being the only daughter".

It must have been very difficult for this family to survive without a breadwinner in those long ago days. We have no details about their early activities, except that meeting of Joanna and Jacob in Brockville. Most of Jacob's educational instructions had been in French or the formal languages of Latin and Greek in the Seminary in Quebec, not the usual language heard in those parts. As a consequence, the new Mrs. Belfry became her new husband's English teacher as well as his wife. Jacob did learn, and was often heard acknowledging Joanna's efforts, which enabled him to "speak plain, intelligent English". They were a spirited couple and quickly settled into life in Brockville where he continued employment in his trade as a cooper.

Jacob carried out his duties as an intelligent, forthright young man who valued his own self worth. He was not overly concerned about the three thousand dollar inheritance from his father's estate (a rather significant amount at that time) that had been frittered away by the executor. Rather, he felt well able to stand on his own feet, and make his own way in the world.

The story is told that once Jacob was working for Mr. Jones, a wealthy flourmill owner in Brockville who required a quantity of barrels. Because Jacob's home was three miles away Mr. Jones invited Jacob to stay for lunch at noon hour. When lunchtime came, Jacob found to his chagrin that he was to be put in the kitchen with the servants rather than dine with the family. When he realized what his status was to be, he returned to the workshop and began packing up his belongings, much to Mr. Jones' distress. Jacob then informed his employer that he considered himself quite equal in training and background, and therefore refused to eat in the kitchen as a menial worker instead of with the family. Mr. Jones, reluctant to lose such a valuable worker, had a quick discussion with his wife, and very soon Jacob took his place at the family dining table where he continued to dine from then on.

Joanna, or Mother Belfry as she was called in later years, was energetic, lively and jovial and became known to all as a fine 'helpmeet' for her husband. She was later to suffer some anxiety during the winter of the 1837 Canadian Rebellion because her son Philo was held in jail for five months, and another son Oran was imprisoned for six weeks in the Presbyterian meetinghouse in Newmarket. She was very worried about her sons, but as the political situation eased, she put the troubles behind her and lived to see her large family marry and settle not far from the family homestead. Indeed, it was rather unusual for parents to have all sixteen of their children, not only survive but also live nearby as they began establishing their own homes and families.

Jacob and Joanna moved a number of times to improve their economic status, and also because of their concern about the activities of the American Revolution.

They lived for a while in New York State near Rochester. Next they moved to Ontario and lived for a while in St Catharines while waiting for a relative from the States to join them. Then they all moved farther north. We can plot their routes somewhat by the registered information regarding their expanding family. The first three of their children were born in the Brockville area:

Children of Jacob and Joanna

1) Oran: b. 5 Feb. 1799 - d. 23 Apr. 1876 in Brockville, Leeds Co.

2) Thirza: b. 25 June 1801 in Brockville, Leeds, Co. - d. 2 Mar. 1860.

3) James: b. 25 Jan. 1803 in Brockville, Leeds, Co. - d. 31 Aug. 1849.

Jacob had a shop in Brockville where they lived at this time and where these children were born.

Their next move was to Elizabethtown where more of their children were born:

4) Mittie: b.16 July 1805 (Submit was her given name) in Elizabethtown Township, Leeds Co. - d. 11 Dec. 1851.

****5) Prince Albert**: b.16 July 1805, and Mittie's twin - d. 12 Mar. 1882.

6) Ira: b.18 Oct.1807 in Elizabethtown Twp, Leeds, Co. - d.18 July 1887.

7) Peter: b.16 Oct. 1809 in Elizabethtown, Twp, Leeds Co. - d. 27 July 1835.

The family then went to the USA where more children were born to this family. Because it was around 1811 and the possibility of war was ever present, a relative of Joanna's persuaded them that they would be safer in the State of New York. That fall of 1811 they took their family, their stock and possessions and moved to Lewiston where they settled at Slusser.

Here another set of twins, a son and a daughter were born.

8) Philo: b. 22 Oct. 1811 in Slusser, Niagara, New York - d.16 April 1885

9) Philana: b. 22 Oc.t 1811 in Slusser, Niagara, New York.

Jacob then moved them further inland to **Genesee Flats,** south of Rochester. This was a fortunate move because soon after they had left, Indians from Canada arrived and killed the family who were dwelling in the home that they had so recently vacated. This move to a large orchard owned by General Wordsworth was good for Jacob. His industrious habits were greatly appreciated by Wordsworth and the two became friends.

Three more children were born there:

10) Joanna; b. 29 July 1813 in Allegany, Genesee, New York.

11) Thomas: b. 8 Sept. 1815 in Allegany, Genesee, N. Y. - d. 27 Jan. 1834.

12) Christopher Columbus: b.18 Sept 1817 in Allegany, Genesee, New York - d. 1895.

Because of the threatening political activities they began to think about a return to Canada after living in the States for seven years. The Genesee Flats had suffered a devastating flood that helped convince the Belfry's to return, settling briefly in St Catharines until Joanna's brother arrived.

Then, as many pioneers were settling in York Twp., they too joined the exodus and went to the township of Markham about 25 miles northeast of Toronto. This location was referred to as 'Little York'. Child number 13 joined them there.

13) William Warren: b. 20 June 1820 in Markham, York Co.

In 1821 Jacob purchased the right to the east half of Lot No. 22 in the 2nd Concession of East Gwillimbury, where the last of the Belfry children were born.

14) Jacob: b. 10 Sept. 1822 in East Gwillimbury, York Co.

15) Clarissa Clara: b. 13 Oct. 1824 in East Gwillimbury, York Co.

16) Catherine: b. 6 May 1826 in East Gwillimbury, York, Co.

By following the dates and birth locations of their family we see that they must have been very busy years with Joanna having a child (or two) every two years as well as tending to her growing family, and moving frequently. The incidence of having twins was to repeat itself in later generations.

Soon after settling in East Gwillimbury, a clearing in the woods was made and a log house was erected. The family lived here for several years until Jacob was able to construct a more impressive dwelling for his wife and their growing family.

Joanna, 'Mother Belfry', made a warm home for her family, and offered a ready welcome to others of the community who wished to visit. She became a caring Methodist, following her early upbringing in the Baptist church, and ministers of all denominations found her home an agreeable resting place for good conversation, intelligent discussion, and gracious hospitality.

By 1845 Father and Mother Belfry had no daughters left at home. The family farm, where the parents and still single son lived, was under the son's management. The son's marriage in March 1846 prompted them to divide the family home so that each family unit was able to use a part of the house for their own requirements.

Mother Belfry had become quite feeble by this time, and now needed to be cared for by a hired attendant. The following year after a brief illness she died at home on 25 August 1847. She was 66 years and 30 days old. She and Jacob had been life partners for over 50 years.

On the death of Joanna, Jacob went to live with his daughter Mittie and her husband, James Aylward, who kept the Post Office in the nearby village of Queensville. It was situated right at the main corner where folks passed by regularly. This suited the gregarious Jacob quite well. Mittie died in 1851 and soon Jacob moved again.

Then Jacob, Father Belfry, sold the homestead to William Cane, a son-in-law who was married to Catharine, or Katie as she was known, and Jacob moved back to the farm, delighted to be living in the place he had spent so many happy days.

Later the farm was again sold, this time to a person not connected to the family, so Jacob moved to son Oran's home just north of Queensville. From then on he continued to go from home to home, always making sure that he was a welcome addition before he moved. This picture of him graces the title page of the book *A Brief History of Jacob Belfry Sen. Compited and Written by P. DeGuerre,* published in Toront in 1888.

For the next few years this was how he lived. He enjoyed being with his nearby sons and daughters and they enjoyed him, so it was a very satisfactory arrangement for all of them. Although he knew he was most welcome he insisted on paying them $1 a week for room and board. He had previously charged others this amount when they were in need of shelter, so it seems that he felt that this was fair remuneration. *(Much of the details of Jacob's life story were recounted to DeGuerre by Oran in his later years. It was said that his excellent recall helped a great deal in accurately recording the family history. It must also be said that Oran died in 1876, more than a decade before this book was printed so quite likely any inaccuracies can be explained by the lapse of time.).*

Jacob liked to rise early, a habit formed in the seminary, and he had been a walker all of his life. Usually he walked to Queensville from his farm very early in the morning, and then off he would go again in the afternoon. He walked not only for his health, but also to maintain the friendships he had formed over the years with others from the community. He was cheerful, warm hearted and friendly so was a welcome visitor in the homes of both relatives and friends. It is said that people enjoyed his visits just as much as he enjoyed visiting them. He kept his stays short, and he and they quite looked forward to the opportunity to be together.

He regularly went north to the Bradford area to see his other children, too. His last trip was to visit his brother William who lived ten miles away. He returned that same evening in good spirits, but seemed to have developed a severe cold and was forced to take to his bed. The family finally insisted on calling a doctor, and concerned members of the family also came. Unfortunately he was unable to rally, and died at Clara and Peter DeGuerre's home on 10 March 1858.

He was 80 years, nine months and nineteen days old. Quite a full interesting, and adventurous life for our patriarch, said to have been born off the Grand Banks of Newfoundland.

Selby Burying Ground with Belfry markers

He is buried in the Selby burying Grounds, York Co., and Joanna is close beside him, as are two of their children.

Peter died at 24 years on 27 July 1835 and Thomas, aged 17 years, died on 27 Jan 1834 of brain fever. This cemetery is at the top of a hill about half a mile north of the present town of Sharon, Ontario. It is a peaceful place with many original stone markers, mute testimony to the energy and forethought of young people who arrived, invested in Crown Land, and settled nearby to make their contribution to our family and others, and indeed to our land.

It is very easy to miss this touching cemetery, which sits at the rise of a hill on a quiet country road, now called Leslie Street. If the trees nearby should be in full leaf, you might not notice the rose-coloured monument peeking out over the hillside. Caring folk have retrieved the markers, grouped them in families, and yes, even placed them on small hillocks so on a clear day it might even be possible to see the peaceful Ontario countryside from their quiet resting places.

Third Generation

Prince Albert, son of Jacob and Joanna, born on July 16, 1805 in Elizabethtown Township, Leeds Co. and the twin brother of Submit (Mittie), is a third generation Belfry, and he is our direct forefather. His trade was listed as a carpenter in the 1881 census. In fact this was a skill that many of his brothers also shared. Prince Albert married Mary Robinson, the daughter of William Robinson, in a ceremony in Coulson's Corners. The Robinson farm was on Lot 15, right next to Prince's on Lot 16 so the families were close and friendly.

William, once the owner of a shoe store in Holland Landing, was one of the first settlers north of Bradford before that town existed. He arrived from King's County, Ireland, in 1822 and later brought his wife and family to the area from Ireland in

1829. The Robinson home soon became a resting place for travellers and early settlers as more people began their new lives in this area. They were a popular, friendly family.

For Prince Albert and Mary's wedding many of those same settlers arrived from around the countryside by oxen and wagons. It was noted that there were 16 yoke of oxen as well as the one horse in the township parked on the William Robinson property during the wedding festivities. It must have been an exciting time, with each new arrival eager for news of other friends, and equally keen to recount their homesteading adventures to each other.

Another Robinson, Peter, lived in the vicinity as well. He built the first grist mill which became very popular as the Red Mill, and it eventually became the nucleus of the village of Newmarket. Historical documents say that a Peter Robinson brought two groups of settlers from the Adare area of Limerick, Ireland, one group of 500 in 1823 and another group in 1825. This later group of 1800 settlers who came in nine ships settled in the Peterborough and Newcastle areas of Ontario. Peter and William's relationship to each other is not known. However, we believe that they were related.

It is interesting to imagine that some of the new settlers could have been connected to our Switzer line, too. In all likelihood messages back and forth between Ireland and Ontario helped to determine where the new arrivals would begin their new lives. Some of those first 'Peter Robinson' settlers were Switzers who found new homes in the Ottawa area. Switzerville, a community near Ottawa was settled by many relatives of Peter Switzer, a relative of our branch.

The sociability of the early settlers did much to bolster their spirits, and it also gave them opportunities to meet all grown-up and marriageable members of other families. In looking at marriage records during those years it is plain to see that many brothers and sisters married sisters, brothers and/or cousins of other neighbouring families.

Prince and Mary settled on Lot 16 (North half), Concession 8 in 1830. His brother Ira settled in the vicinity, too, and it was on Ira's property that one of the first burying grounds for the town of Bradford was created. This small cemetery is still in evidence near Bradford. The stones have been grouped together in families and this sign proclaims it as The Belfry M. E. Cemetery. The initials stand for Methodist Episcopal, Bradford West Gwillimbury.

The name Prince is an unusual one. Historians feel that he could have been named after Joanna's brother, by the same name and/or her father, also Prince. Some historians also use the spelling 'Prence'. Another suggestion was that the name might be a contraction of Prince-town, the first place of landing in 1620 of the Puritan Pilgrims. The 10 November 1620 arrival of the *Mayflower* in Princetown Rock was certainly an historic event, followed by the final landing at Plymouth Rock on 22 December 1620. In subsequent generations we still can see that the names 'Prince', 'Sherman' and 'Joanna' are frequently used in the Belfry connection, attesting to the significant regard in which these forefathers were held.

<u>The children of Prince and Mary were</u>:

<u>Jacob</u>**: b. 4 March 1835 - d. 31 Jan. 1912, burial in Union Cemetery, Victoria Harbour, m. **Elizabeth Martin** on 25 Dec 1861 (b. 9 June 1836 - d. 1913)

Eliza: b. 1837, m. John Woods

Peter: b. 1840 – d. 1882, m. Isabelle Tapper and 2) Letitia Love

George Robinson: b. 1844 - m. Alice Jean Mackie

William: b. 1845 - remained single

James: b. about 1847 - m Mary Ellsworth

Joanna: b. 1851 -

Henry Stiles: b. 1853 – about 1901, m. Maria Glassford, b. 1854 – d. about 1901.

Prince Albert: b. 1856 - remained single

As well as clearing and cultivating the land, Prince, a carpenter by trade, built an ashery for making potash, giving revenue and employment to his clan.

When the lye ashes were strong enough, they were boiled down and melted into potash. He then took his barrels of potash to Toronto, and loaded them onto vessels heading to Montreal via Lake Ontario and the St. Lawrence River. At times he even took the barrels to Montreal himself. This was quite an undertaking at that time, and the impressive sum of $600 per load realized from this enterprise helped him to pay for his farm and educate his large family.

Prince was a Reformer and took keen interest in the politics of the day. He and his wife were Methodists and their home was a frequent stop for ministers visiting in the area who needed a quiet resting place and pleasant conversation.

On 14t March in the year 1882, Prince rode ten miles to visit his brother, William. That same evening he returned to his home, ate dinner and then retired at his usual time. His wife Mary arose first the next morning and made breakfast. Then she

went to call him, and to her shock and dismay, she found that he had died in his sleep.

Twelve days later she, too, passed away -- a tremendous shock to their family and friends. They were a loving couple as is noted on their gravestone inscription in Mount Pleasant Cemetery in Bradford, Ontario: "*They were lovely and pleasant in their lives and by their death they were not long divided.*"

Tombstone of Prince and Mary Belfry, Mount Pleasant Cemetery, Bradford, Ontario

Peter DeGuerre, the writer of the family history had been a classmate (winter of 1840-41) of four of the younger Belfry children. The school they attended was located at the four corners of the present village of Queensville. As mentioned previously De Guerre became the husband of Clarrisa, also known as Clara, one of the youngest Belfry daughters. Because he was a friend and brother-in-law they freely recounted the stories that families tell each other about their activities, their dreams and their concerns. Thus we have this anecdotal picture of the large gregarious Belfry family.

A Community Grows

The exact date of the first Queensville pioneers is not known but a school building had been constructed there by the mid 1820's. The first teacher, Mr. James Aylward (born 1797 in England), came from Wexford, Ireland to Canada in 1822 after teaching in Aghade, Ireland. Next he taught in Scarborough, coming to East Gwillimbury in 1826 to continue his profession. He taught in Queensville for five more years and then became a businessman. James Aylward would have been well established here when Prince and Mary arrived in 1830. Quite likely they would have approved when Mr. Aylward married Mittie Belfry (1805), Prince's twin sister. He operated the first store in the village and later was postmaster in the first Post Office that began operating 21 May 1851. The Post Office was located in Mr. Aylward's own home.

Former Queensville Post Office, the Aylward House

It was a large double house on the southwest corner of the Queen Street-Queensville Side road. A village dressmaker also had a popular shop there where she fashioned clothing for the ladies of the hamlet. Soon stagecoaches passed by, inns and hotels sprung up, and flour and gristmills and other businesses began to make their appearances. No doubt the Belfry family watched with fascination as this new community came to life.

Unfortunately Mittie took some kind of fever and died in her 47th year on 11 December 1851. Mr. Aylward later married a second time, but had no issue and died on 17 February 1875.

DeGuerre tells us that the first temperance society in the section was organized the summer of 1843. The younger Belfry boys and girls and other friends from the surrounding area took a large wagon of supporters to a community rally in Newmarket. They loved to sing, and often were found singing and socializing in the Belfry home where the cheerful, friendly family encouraged them.

That summer a new name for the hamlet was under discussion. Clara suggested Queensville after Queen Victoria, who as a recently crowned and popular young monarch was making her subjects proud of their heritage. After some discussion this was the name decided upon. In order to publicize their new name, a huge wagon with extended seats on each side was constructed and the name Queensville Band was painted on each side. This in turn was driven around the countryside with its group of eager young musicians. One imagines them perched on the wagon, singing lustily to publicize their new locality. The name stuck and was soon accepted as fact. And Queensville it still remains.

Most of the Belfry children settled a few miles away from their parents' home, quite an interesting fact given that the whole area was quickly spreading out to other parts of what we now call Ontario. They did find much pleasure in being close enough for frequent visits. Grandchildren were born and grew up. Some stayed near by, some went to other parts of Ontario, and still other went to the States. Some farmed, some went into the grocery business, and there were harness makers, mill hands, teachers and doctors.

There is quite a large well kept cemetery just north of Queensville and this is where Submit and her husband, James, are buried, as well as Oran and his wife, and Catharine, and her husband, Peter Moore, and their two daughters.

Jacob Belfry, Our Great-Great-Grandfather

Here we follow another Jacob Belfry, a namesake of our first Jacob. Because we are primarily interested in chronicling our immediate line, we'll zero in on Jacob who was the oldest child of Prince and Mary, and who is our great-grandfather. Following each new generation is an interesting task as it helps to plot how and where they developed new roots. Jacob (b. King Township, York Co., 4 Mar 1835 - d. 31 Jan 1912, West Gwillimbury, Simcoe Co., Ont.) and his wife, Elizabeth Martin, (b. 9 June 1836, (King Twp., York Co., Ont.), married on 25 Dec. 1861, decided to move toward Georgian Bay and settle there. This was becoming a popular area with good Crown land offered to interested homesteaders.

Fourth Generation

The children of Jacob and Elizabeth were:

****Prince Sherman**: b.1863, m. **Esther Ellen Ney**, 25 Nov. 1889 - d. Owen Sound, 1952: our ancestors

Phoebe Jane: b.1864 - d.15 Dec., 1948, m. George Crooke on 18 Jan. 18

George Henry: b.1866 - ??, m. Ann Jane Russell on 6 Feb. 1889

John Wesley: b. about 1868 – ??, m. Phoebe Ann Hazelton on 24 Dec. 1890

Joseph Albert: b.1870, m. Martha Maude Ney on 26 Dec. 1894, sister of Esther - d. 30 Jan. 1958

William James: b.1871 - d. 6 Mar. 1891 (killed by falling tree)

Mary Elizabeth: b. 27 Jan. 1873, m. William Crooke 23 Dec. 1810 - d. 1955

Charlotte Matilda: b.1876 - ??

Jacob Andrew: b. 1879, m. Ellen Morris, 1881 - d.1999

*Esther and Maude Ney were sisters and George and William Crooke were brothers.

Jacob, Elizabeth and son William's tombstone in Midland Cemetery

Arnim Belfry, a grandson of Jacob and Elizabeth, wrote a fascinating account of this family that appeared in a Midland newspaper in January 1950 in order that the original settlers of the village of Vasey, Ont., could be recognized. I will borrow liberally from his first-hand account.

Arrnim wrote that there were four original settlers who travelled together up the old Penetang Road from Bradford in July 1863. They were Jacob and his wife, Elizabeth (Martin), Jacob's brothers Peter and George and a friend, Benjamin Mackie. Mackie settled on Lot 1, Concession V, Tay Township, Jacob took the next lot north, the west half of Lot 2, Concession IV, Peter chose the west half Lot 1 concession IV and George chose the east half of Lot 1, Concession IV. They were close enough to each other for company but all had ample room to grow.

The first important task was the building of their dwellings. Their roofs were constructed using split hollow basswood logs in two layers, one facing up and one facing down. We can only imagine the difficulties they faced. Certainly they were totally without any of the conveniences that we take for granted.

No plumbing, no stores near by, and one can imagine that their tools were not of the latest design. And probably one of the most difficult aspects of all, especially for Elizabeth, was the inability to have frequent visits with absent relatives.

Jacob was the only one of the four who was married, and he and his Elizabeth were the proud parents of six-month-old son, **Prince Sherman**, our grandfather.

When Sherman's sister Phoebe arrived a year later in 1864 she became the first white child to be born in the vicinity of Vasey. The nearest neighbours lived four miles away and their only contact with civilization was by Indian and/or lumberman trails to Waverley. No telephones for them. What a long cold winter it must have been with two very young children in their newly constructed log cabin.

Great Grandmother Belfry lived in the community for six months without even seeing another woman. Then an Indian lady was her first visitor. What an experience that must have been! One wonders just how they communicated. We can imagine that, along with a cup of tea, a good deal of hand signs about the two lively children and their antics were served that day.

Soon the family of Robert Webb, who had grown daughters, arrived to live on the lot north of Jacob and Elizabeth's property. These new arrivals must have greatly pleased Elizabeth. Then the Brown, Robinson, Simpson, Hall and Vasey families followed. Soon a new community was born and eventually was called Vasey, quite likely after its first postmaster (*Historical data taken from the old Family Bible owned by Joe Belfry, a brother of Prince Sherman, who lived in Midland, Ont.).*

The Prince Sherman Belfry family gradually enlarged to include five more brothers and two more sisters. As in other beginning communities, their logging-bees, barn-raisings, quilting-bees, and old time dances quickly knit these homesteaders into a cohesive group.

Russell's School at Vasey provided what little formal education these children received.

By 1880 the family moved to another farm near Victoria Harbour. They worked hard to cut trees for their home and furniture. By their early teens the boys were able to share in these tasks.

But there was always time for fun. It seems that getting together with others remained at the core of the family's social activities well after these initial parties. I well remember Christmas happenings in Midland when cousins, uncles, aunts and grandparents all sang and danced together through the evening, revelling in being together and having a glorious time. I also remember trying to sort out who was who, as many folks from the Ney, Taylor and Belfry families had married cousins and/or siblings, creating an "I'm my own grandpa" syndrome.

On paper it is reasonably clear, but when real people are involved it gets a little more complicated it seems. But, oh, we did have fun when we got together as I expect the early generations did as well.

And they grew.

In due time Prince Sherman met a lovely lass named Esther Ellen Ney and they married on 25 November, 1889 in Tay Township, Simcoe. They are our beloved grandparents. Esther's parents also came to Canada from Ireland, but from the Cavan area, not Limerick. Before we hear about the life that she and Sherman created it might be interesting to know a little bit about Esther's forefathers and about their arrival.

The Ney Family

The first records we have been able to find of the Ney family begin with the following genealogical data.

Robert Ney (1728-1786) and **Sarah?**(1736-1786), gave birth to our first Ney ancestor but we have no other data about their lives.

So we will begin our part of this family story with **Robert Ney: b. 1776,** possibly a grandson, who married **Margaret: b. 1780**, married in 1799. Both were from County Cavan, and became the parents of **Robert John Ney**, b.1805 - d.1849, our ancestor.

Records from baptismal records in Drung Parish, County Cavan provide these statistics about their family.

Children of Robert and Margaret:

Elizabeth: b. 7 Feb. 1801, Drung Parish, County Cavan, Ireland
William: b. 2 Nov. 1802, Drung Parish, County Cavan, Ireland
James: b. 27 Dec. 1804, Drung Parish, County Cavan, Ireland;
****John**: b 28 Oct. 1806 Drung Parish - d. I Jan. 1850, Port Darlington On.
Frances: b. 22 Dec. 1811, Drung Parish, County Cavan, Ireland
Robert: b. 28 Sept. 1813, Drung Parish, County Cavan, Ireland

Alexander: b. 25 March 1816, Drung parish, County Cavan, Ireland
Margaret: b. 6 Dec. 1818, Drung Parish, County Cavan, Ireland - d. 6 De. 1818 Drung Parish, County Cavan, Ireland

John: (b.1806) m. **Jane Wilson**, (b.1809 in Drung, Cavan) in 1838 in Knockbride, Cavan, Ireland. Jane died in 1890, in Durham Ontario.

John and his wife, Jane, along with four sons and a daughter came to Canada in 1849 from the community of Knockbride near Cavan in Ireland. One of the special possessions John brought to Canada was a letter from the parish rector of the Church of England at Knockbride.

This "*to whom it might concern*," document was written by Rector Guy L'Estrange, who served the parish from 1842 - 1852.

In it he attested to John's good character and hoped that anyone with whom John had dealings would treat him with generosity. One assumes that this form of introduction must have been the 1849 version of our present day passports.

An article in a 1949 Midland Ontario paper entitled "Ney Family Celebrates" gives some details about this particular possession prior to a reunion of John and Jane's descendents. The document in question has its own story.

This character reference only reached John Neay after he had already set sail. The article states: "*The little schooner on which they began their journey apparently ran into a dense fog as they began their sixteen-week crossing of the Atlantic. When the fog finally lifted, the little ship was practically back where it started, just off the Irish coast. It was then that a small yacht hove to alongside the schooner and the captain of the schooner was asked if he had a John Neay aboard.*

Answering in the affirmative, the captain was given the following letter to hand to his passenger";

"We whose names are undersigned do certify that the bearer, John A. Neay was born and bred in the Parish of Knockbride, in the County of Cavan, Ireland and that he is descended of very respectable parents and that he has always behaved as a sober, religious and industrious young man. He purposes to immigrate to the lands of America. We do therefore recommend him to the patronage of all gentlemen and religious and well-disposed persons, under whom God in his gracious providence may cause his lot to be cast.

Given under our hands this 8th day of May, 1849"

Rector, Guy L'Estrange, Knockbride, Ireland

The 'a' in the name Neay was dropped sometime in subsequent years.

It is interesting that the newspaper account after that 1949 Midland reunion reported, "*Following supper, races, sports, and a special get together rounded out the program.*" These picnics and get-togethers were joyous occasions and all ages took pleasure at being together. Great shouts of joy, happy greetings and mounds of wonderful food also accompanied the happenings. What wonderful survivors.

Just imagine the anguish of having to set out *again* from the fog-shrouded Irish coast after a tearful good-bye. The paseengers must have been weary, discouraged but resigned to begining once more. Hopefully, receiving this document absorbed some of the sting that this postponement created.

Imagine life aboard a schooner with five small children, likely very poor facilities and little food or conveniences. Would it be preferable to the option of living in a famine swept land? What difficult, impossible questions. One can only guess that leaving must have been the best solution available at the time. And we could well reflect on how we tend to bemoan the six or so hours it now takes us to fly to Europe.

John and Jane's children were children were:
George b. 1839 - d.1922, m. Margaret Madill, b.1844 - d.1930, ** our great grandfather
Robert: b.1840 - d.1923, m. Elizabeth Van Camp, b.1856 - 1918
William: b.1842 - d.1923, m. Eliza Jane Wilson, b.1869 - 1939
Margaret Jane: b. 844 - d.1930, m. Robert J. Wilson, b.1868 - 1948
John: b. 1846 - d.1931, m. Charlotte Atkinson, b.1863 - 1932
Thomas: b.1849 - d.1931, m. Ann Elizabeth Smith, b.1856 - d.1936
(We note that several of the Wilsons and Neys intermarried down through the years)

As it happened I was given my grandmother's copy of the fascinating document carried by John Ney while teaching, so that it could be used as a hands-on teaching tool. Not only was it used as such, I held it in my hand as we headed to Cavan on the first day of a trip to Ireland in 2000 when we started our own search for family roots.

Ireland had always held a certain fascination for me because so many family stories began there, so we eagerly headed cross-country to see where this forefather had lived. Historic places were visited en route, like Drogheda, site of the 1690 Battle of the Bulge. For years we had heard about the Battle of the Bulge but until then had no knowledge of where it was or what happened. We saw a Viking encampment, circa 911 A.D., and beautiful Celtic crosses and round towers. As we explored, we marveled at the beautiful countryside, the spring blossoms and the lovely wee villages.

Miles flew by, and as night was beginning to fall I spied a small arrow pointing off the main road just before reaching our destination, Cavan. The sign said, 'Knockbride'! We were amazed, as despite much searching, the little village had not appeared on our map. What excitement. Too late in the day to try to stop then, but that certainly was of high priority for the next day's itinerary.

After visiting the Genealogy Offices in Cavan next morning, we established that Neays had lived in the area and records verified Rector L'Estrange's ten-years at Knockbride.

Next we eagerly headed back to see if we could find the sign, and the church. Yes, the sign was there and a few miles down that road, there stood the old stone Knockbride Church of Ireland that we had sought.

Wandering silently through the adjoining cemetery, we read the headstones that recounted the lives of those whose last resting place it was. Names and dates carved in stone told the history of whole families who had been wiped out during the famine years. What a devastating time it must have been. Soon I realized that these headstones carried familiar names of so many Southern Ontario families. Names like, Kincaid, Parr, Johnson, Mahood, and Wilson were only a few of the names we knew. Was Wilson the same family from which John's wife Jane came? How poignant to think of all those families and their history.

Knockbride Church of Ireland, Cavan, Ireland

As with other significant stops on heritage adventures, we were quite humbled by imagining the courage needed to leave one's homeland and seek a new land. Courageously this family bundled up their growing family in the summer of 1849, and with Jane, who was pregnant, took children and belongings and set off for a new life. What boldness it must have taken. Following the sea voyage they landed in Port Hope and soon settled near Blackstock in Ontario.

Sadly John fell ill and died on 1st of January 1850, shortly after son Thomas had joined their family the previous fall. Jane was left with a new baby and five other children, the eldest of which, our forefather George, was only ten years old. Fortunately a cousin in Port Darlington was able to give her much help but one wonders how she had the fortitude to continue.

But the children, as well as other family members, pulled together to assist them. Now we will continue with the life and times of their first son George, our great-grandfather, who is our link to this family. George married Margaret Madill and became the parents of our grandmother and a number of other children.

George and Margaret's children were:
Eliza Jane: b.1866 - d. 1889, Cartwright Township, Durham West
Thomas George: b.1868, Cartwright Township, Durham West - d.1944
John: b. 7 May 1870 – d. before 1881, Cartwright Township, West Durham
Margaret Ann: b. 7 May 1870, Cartwright Township, Durham West - d. 28 March, 1932, Deloraine, Manitoba., m. **William Mackie ,** b. 8 March 1865 – d. 1935, who was accused of her death. John and Margaret appear to be twins
****Esther Ellen**: b.16 May 1872, Cartwright Township, Durham West - d.13 Nov. 1963, Victoria Harbour, m. 25 Nov. 1891 **Sherman Belfry** in Midland. Our grandmother and grandfather!
Robert William: b.14 Feb. 1874, Cartwright Township, Durham, d. 1963. William was the last blacksmith in Midland, Ontario; m. Jean Stephenson before 1975.
Martha Maud: b. 20 May 1876 - d.1958, married **Joe Belfry**, b.1870 - d.1958,
m. Joseph Belfry, brother of Sherman on 26 Dec. 1895
Charlotte Edna: b. 6 June 1877, Cartwright Township, Durham – d. about 1965, Stayner, Ont., m **William Collins** b. 1867 – d. 1953
John James: b. 1878 - d.1966, Cartwright Township, Durham, married **Eva Taylor**, b.1887 - d.1963, sister of Lu, Viola and Emily
Mary Elizabeth: b. 4 Oct. 1881, Cartwright Township, Durham, – d. 1932, Midland, m. 1 Oct. 1902 Wesley Newborn on, b. 21 Dec. 1876
Mabel: b. 17 April 1883, Cartwright Township, Durham d. 1958 Midland, married 14 June 1905 **William Hook** b. 23 Sept. 1874 d. 16 June 1925 Midland.
Leslie Joseph: b. 13 Feb. 1884, Cartwright Township Durham, - d 1975, m. 26 April 1913, **Viola Taylor**, b.1890 - d.1971, sister of Lu and Emily

Ney brothers and sisters from left: John Ney, Mabel Hook, Les Ney, Edna Collins, Maud Belfry, Esther Belfry (our Grandmother), and Will Ney

Most of these members of the Belfry/Ney family remained in southern Ontario, except for Margaret, who married William Mackie and went west around 1892. They resided on a farm near Deloraine, Manitoba, for a while, and later moved near Hazeldean. News accounts speak of her involvement in United Church and community activities. She was the mother of five sons and four daughters. For some unknown reason in March 1932, Wm Mackie murdered his wife in the parlour of their home and then went for police to inform them of the situation. This shocked the community and very much saddened her many friends and relatives. No explanation was made as to the reason this happened but he was taken to gaol. Later one of his sons reported that his father had died in Brandon Asylum for the criminally insane.

Our grandparents, Sherman Belfry and Esther Ney, were wedded on Nov 25 1891 at the Presbyterian Manse in Midland. Their attendants were Sherman's brother Joe Belfry and Esther's sister Maude Ney, who later also married. As it happened, both these couples lived long, happy lives and both celebrated more than 50 years of marriage. They remained very good friends and were frequently at the picnics and parties held by the clan.

Sherman and Esther, or Essie as she was called, settled on a farm near Victoria Harbour. They remained there while bringing up their family. The farm was an exciting place to visit. Some of the older grandchildren remember the farmhouse with its surprising trap door in the pantry that led to the cold, earth cellar and bins of winter vegetables. The well outside was a source of fascination too because one could bring up icy cold water by the dipperful, but there was also another attraction. There was a shelf just above the water line and on it, being cooled, was the freshly churned butter, the milk and the cream. Such treasures!

One concession away from the Belfry's but easily reached by shortcut across the fields, lived a family by the name of Taylor who had nine girls and one son. These Taylor and Belfry children all went to Newtonville School so it was a perfect situation for life long friendships and marriages. Lula and Emily Taylor married Norman's brothers, Roy and Arnim, and their sister Alzina married Eldon, a Belfry cousin.

In the Ney family, Essie's brothers Leslie and John also married two of the other Taylor sisters, Viola and Eva. Just to complicate things further Essie's sister Maude married Sherman's brother Joseph. For years all of these families visited back and forth and we were never quite sure how we were related. Suffice it to say that it didn't matter much as everyone was congenial and welcoming.

<u>Sherman and Esther's children and spouses are as follows:</u>
Sherman Roy: b. 24 April 1993 – d. 5 Jan. - 1961 m. **Lula Anne Taylor**, b.11 Sept. 1895 - 31 Mar. 1977 on 15 Oct. 1922.
Laura Myrtle: b.10 Sept. 1894 - 13 Mar. 1973, m. **Linus Vasey (**b. 7 Jan 1889 - d. 1976) on 9 Oct. 1924.
Melville Lawrence: b.11 May 1896 - 26 June 1948, m. **Olive Miller** C, (b. 23 July 1905 - d. 31 Oct. 1991)
Arnim Earl: b. 19 Mar. 1898 - d. 12 Mar. 1984, m. **Emily Taylor (**b.18 Nov. 1898 - d.14 Aug. 14 1991) on 28, 1924
<u>Norman Ambrose</u>: b. 21 Sept. 1899 - d. 8 July 1974, m. **<u>Mary Margurite Hillis (</u>**b. Feb. 27 1907 - d. 25 Sept. 2000) on Nov 13, 1928 (our parents)
Merton Linwood: b.20 May 1901 - d. 28 July 1978, m. **Margaret Ferrier** (b.1905 - d. 14 Oct 1990) on 2 Sept. 1940
George Orin: b. 10 April 1913 - d. April 6 1979, m. 1) **Marion Braden**, (b.1915 - d. 2 June 1973)
2) **Olive Miller Belfry**: b. 1905 - d.1990, on 27 July 1975, widow of Melville Lawrence Belfry
Dorothy Eileen: born to the Molineaux family in Coldwater, adopted 1915 - d. 5 April 1946, m. **Fred Rumney**, (b. 1905 - d.1966)

By these dates we can see that when Orin was born the older boys were pretty much grown up. Our grandparents, Sherman and Essie, were still living on the farm and were concerned that he would be lonely, so they adopted a sweet little daughter named Dorothy for a playmate.

Dorothy's family, who lived in Coldwater, already had a number of children and another baby was going to be a serious financial strain. As I recall, they kept in touch with her first family, the Molineaux, sharing both financial and emotional bonds that allowed Dorothy to know and love both of her families and other siblings. A wonderful bond developed between Orin and Dorothy. They were kindred spirits and they treasured their affection all of their lives.

The Sherman Belfrys

Back row: Orin, Mert, Arnim, Laura, Mel, Roy, Norm
Front row: Sherman Belfry, Esther Ney Belfry, and Dorothy Belfry

These boys and girls are Norman's siblings and thus became an integral part of life for Mary and Norm and for their heirs of which we are a part.

We will meet the women they married, see where they shared their lives, and hear how they continually made opportunities to be together in large groups to celebrate, or in small captured moments to just sit and visit.

Because these are our uncles and aunts, we have heard many of their stories, some from listening to them recounted with glee, some from the story chair, and some found their way into mother Mary's diaries over the years. They were a cheerful bunch of men and women who just seemed to light up when around each other. As we will see, not only their choice of vivacious partners but the similarity of their chosen area of work drew them close as well.

'The Boys' as the older ones were called all went to school usually when the farm work was done in the fall. They were a handsome bunch, and grew strong and healthy. These bright, feisty boys laughed often and always enjoyed playing pranks on each other. The opportunity for advanced schooling was not open to them at that time but they were lifetime learners and took night and corresponding courses as well as work-related training at every opportunity. They also read everything in sight during their working lives and at leisure, just for the sheer joy of acquiring knowledge.

While they were young men at home they worked hard, too. They loved to tell about walking the several miles into Victoria Harbour and then heading across the CPR railway bridge to their work in the grain elevator in Port McNicoll. In the winter when that part of Georgian Bay was frozen they delighted in racing to work across the ice. Many times when they finished their jobs late in the day they found to their surprise that the ice had melted, so it was back to the tracks for them. How they laughed to tell about it but we imagine they must have often tempted all the fates by continuing that dangerous practice.

We will begin their part of this story by looking at the life that their eldest son, **Sherman Roy** made for himself. Although he carried the traditional name of Sherman, no doubt after his father and with a nod to Joanna's long-gone relatives, he was known as Roy all his life. Roy began his Hydro career at Waubaushene, Ont. In the summer of 1914 he worked on the construction of transmission lines to provide hydropower for the area. This was before there were regular hours or holidays with pay so Roy worked both Christmas and New Year's Day that year. It must have left a noticeable hole in his family circle. Those of us who know the history of this family in Hydro circles are rather awed by the happenstance that would motivate so many others to follow in Roy's footsteps.

Roy Belfry

He began a kind of 'Belfry dynasty' in the Ontario Hydro. We will hear that his siblings and theirs have popped up in ever widening Hydro circles for nearly 100 years. Was it because their family was just starting to grow into manhood at the time this commodity was in its infancy?

Certainly Roy, as the eldest brother, was very special in the eyes of his siblings, so perhaps they just were following their hero. We will follow them, too, and see how the family, and the company, developed.

If we were to glance at the world's political situation at that time we would see that a serious threat to world peace was taking place across the Atlantic.

The First World War (1914-1918) was in progress and many countries were gripped with anxiety. So, along with a host of like minded men, in Feb.1916 Roy enlisted, and by that July he was a soldier on active duty in France. The few months between enlisting and being jettisoned into the heart of battle makes one realize that these young men were placed in war zones with very little military training. Quite a frightening thought! His brother Melville, who was only 18, followed in Roy's footsteps as well. How Grandma Belfry must have worried.

Roy and Melville Belfry

In an Easter letter Roy sent to his mother from Bramshop Camp, Bexhill on the Sea, Hants, England, on 17 March 1918 he voiced his worries about the lack of news about Melville. He also shared some of the horror of the famous battle of Vimy Ridge where Canadian troops put forth such amazing efforts to thwart the almost impenetrable German stronghold.

Roy says: *"I remember last Easter well. I was in the trenches then and we were going over the top at daybreak the next morning. That was when the battle of Vimy Ridge started. I remember I sent you a field card and wondered if it would be my last. We knew it could be the last day for a lot of us but I was one of the lucky ones, and I came through without a scratch. We were a proud lot that night. We held the ridge that Fritz had held all through the war. When I get home I will tell you what it was like. It was worth being in it and if I live to be a hundred I will remember it as if it was yesterday"*

Uncle Roy did talk about that harrowing experience in the years that followed. He told of some of their discussions while waiting for action in muddy trenches. Would it be better to remain with feet down, or should they keep their heads above, they wondered. What life altering decisions must have been called for on a daily basis, especially when the enemy was mere yards away! It is poignant to imagine them weighing the pros and cons of survival. Was any spot in those dangerous places safe? Roy chose to stand up in the trench so that his head was out that day, and lived to tell about it. Some of his friends made the other choice and were not so lucky.

The enemy trenches were so close that they must have been able to see the expression in the faces of their foes. How did anyone survive that carnage? There were well over ten thousand Canadian casualties, among them 3,598 deaths.

Trenches at Vimy circa 1992

One participant recalled the din of a thousand guns and a flaming hillside. Some of those images of war must have been burnt into their minds forever. What a horror it must have been.

On the site of Vimy Ridge a soaring monument now stands guard as a haunting reminder of that pivotal battle. Many, many young Canadians died there that Easter Sunday of 1917. And many untried German youth did as well. This monument was dedicated by a newly crowned King Edward VIII on July 26, 1936. It was said that our country, still in its infancy, came of age and gained true independence during this battle.

Our uncle was left with a sad souvenir from that battle. Mustard gas, a dreadful new weapon was in use by the enemy, and those who breathed the vapours ran the risk of death or severe damage to their lungs. Unfortunately Uncle Roy's lungs were badly affected, and he suffered for the rest of his life from serious breathing problems.

Roy Belfry and Lulu Taylor Belfry

Later Roy and his wife Lula (Taylor) lived for many years in a large home in Cannington, Ontario, and his struggle for breath was a frequent companion. Ultimately it was to be the cause of his death, as he choked to death in his home, helpless, and unable to call Aunt Lu, who was in another part of their home.

Roy frequently regaled us with stories of being in Europe, and often at family parties his favourite smelly Limburger cheese held a place of honour on the table. The rest of us looked on in amazement as he relished every morsel of that pungent dish. He loved the foods he sampled in France and was delighted to journey back to Vimy with Aunt Lu for the opening celebrations and dedication of this impressive monument.

Environmental effects over the generations caused serious disintegration to the Vimy memorial, but in this year of 2007 it has been once again returned to its former splendour and rededicated to the sacrifice of so many soldiers whose gift of life helped to keep Canada strong and free.

It is a magnificent edifice, mounted proudly on the ridge overlooking the now verdant French countryside. Standing beside that breathtaking work of art is a profoundly moving experience. No, we must not forget!

A few random lines from an anonymous poem found among Mary's paper tell of the personal anguish felt in our land:

Farmers tarry yet awhile
'Ere you sow on Vimy plain.
Let the earth regain her smile,
Let the song birds sing again,
Leave the harvest. God will reap.
Canada the price has paid
Let our tired comrades sleep.
You must do no reaping there.

The Vimy Memorial

Roy and Aunt Lu never had children of their own, but they were enthusiastic uncles and aunts. They liked having children around and always made us feel very special when we were with them.

Roy returned to Canada after the war and again he joined the Hydro as a member of a construction crew. By 1926 he arrived in Cannington as a one-man crew: superintendent, construction lineman, operating lineman, meter reader and maintenance man. Whew!

Farms in that rich agricultural community were still using coal oil and manpower, but the Ontario Hydro stepped in to change the lives of many by building power lines along those picturesque country roads.

No forestry crews were there to clear the roadsides, no heavy equipment helped them fell the trees, drag the poles through the forest, or haul them to the site. Teams of horses with wagons or sleighs, depending on the weather, were required for this next step. Finally, after backbreaking effort was expended, the post-holes were dug by the work crew, and then huge poles were carefully raised upright and installed, thanks to two or three, brawny men.

The installation of power lines and transformers required many more steps before electricity brightened the lives of rural farmers. And Uncle Roy made sure that it was done properly.

The next time you drive along a country road, look up and consider the man-hours that were needed to bring electric power to the farms of this country in those early years. Over the next decades Roy was at the helm in snow, sleet or thunderstorm. As he was well known, he was always the first one called in a crisis, and he always accompanied his men to a trouble site regardless of the weather. The foregoing account of his work history, paraphrased from an article in the *Cannington Gleaner,* Vol. 96, No. 44 1967, was written by Islay Lambert, his office assistant for many years and a good friend of the family. Islay often was included in Roy and Lu's social activities and family gatherings and was an involved member of the community. Her thoughtful article reminded readers that those who died in the trenches were not the only heroes of the war. The many veterans who returned home to their families readily shouldered the challenge of helping Canada grow into a country of which they and their fallen comrades could be proud.

Uncle Roy and Aunt Lu's attic was home to the huge steamer trunk that they had used on their visit back to Europe. It was stored there in a corner, and what a cache of treasures it guarded! There were enormous hats, frilly scarves, swishy dresses, purses, and feather boas. It was such fun to get all decked out in these vintage fashions and parade around with our finery. What a delightful way to spend a Sunday afternoon when visiting them in Cannington, not far from our Uxbridge home.

Once during a power black out while we were visiting, Aunt Lu sent her dinner casserole to a Mrs Lee who lived next door to be cooked on her wood stove. Dinner had been devoured, when Uncle Roy, with a gleam in his eye, asked Mary if she had like enjoyed the rabbit stew. Mary was outraged. The very idea of eating rabbit! Most likely it was chicken but Uncle Roy's hearty laugh filled the room. How he liked to tease.

Sister **Laura** married Linus Vasey who lived near the Taylors and Belfrys. When their sons, Jerry, Garnet and Mark, and daughter, Nelda, were of school age they moved into Victoria Harbour, and we often visited them there when we were young. I remember staying overnight with our cousins and hearing our brothers shout while listening to the Saturday night hockey games.

The radio was turned to full volume and the rafters fairly shook with cheers when Foster Hewitt shouted, "He shoots! He scores!!" Then hoots and whistles took over as the boys expressed their joy. Needless to say, our brothers were jubilant and hockey continued to be important to them for years.

Linus Vasey and Laura Belfry Vasey during a family holiday in Parry Sound, 1948

Melville Lawrence appeared as the next of the Belfry sons. He arrived on 11 May 1895. In 1915 he, too, enlisted in the army and served for four years. He also saw action in Europe. No doubt the example of his older brother helped in his decision to enlist. It must have been very difficult for their parents to have two sons on European soil with their lives in peril. After the war Melville, Mel as he was called, worked for a time with Bell Telephone Co. in Toronto.

Mel and Olive Miller Belfry

Then the lure of Hydro convinced him to start with the Operating Department of the Hydro as a lineman in 1925. While on the job in Beaverton he stayed at the only hotel in town and met Olive Miller who was working in the dining room. Their first date was a double date with Fred Balcombe, a fellow lineman and his date. It seems that sparks flew because Mel and Olive became engaged and were married in Victoria Harbour on June 28th, 1928. They were blessed with two daughters, Doris and Leona, now known as Lee.

Mel and his family then moved to Severn Falls, after which he became line patrolman at Barrie. In 1931 he was promoted to Line Superintendent at Markdale and later District Line Foreman. They lived for a number of years in Markdale, Ontario, and summers often found them sharing holidays with sibling, aunts and cousins.

Here they are visiting us in the garden of our new home in Uxbridge.

Norm, Olive and Mel, Lee and Marg in Norm and Mary's back yard in Uxbridge

Brother **Arnim Earl** was the next son in line. When Arnim was about 14 years old, he was taken to the doctor where his parents were told that his heart was not strong. Arnim's children think that the doctor must have suspected rheumatic fever, but whatever was the case, the prescription was to stay in bed for a year. This was not a fun thing to do, but Grandma Belfry felt it was necessary for Arnim's health, so it was done.

Arnim as a teenager

That was a long year, but with an interesting result. Arnim became an avid reader. In fact, we understand that he read the whole of the Bible during that long year.

Likely there was a short supply of fresh reading material in their home as there were no stores nearby, but families did have Bibles. Arnim loved to read and this interest remained all his life. And his knowledge and fascination in the Bible stayed with him for life.

Arnim was the second son to come under the spell of one of the Taylor girls. He met his wife-to-be, Emily, and a sister of Lula, when they all went to school together at the Newtonville School on the corner of the Taylor farm. Arnim and Emily married on June 28, 1924 in Durham, Ontario with Lu and Roy as their witnesses. Their first move was to Eugenia Valley where power lines were being installed and then to Hanover in early 1925. This is where their first daughter, Gloria Esther, was born. It is also where the Hillis and Belfry families were to begin their lifelong link.

Arnim and Emily Belfry in the early years of marriage

Arnim and Emily and wee Gloria moved back to Eugenia in 1926 where life was full of outdoor activities for their growing family. Donald was the next child born to

Arnim and Emily. The family continued to grow to include Marjory, and then June. These siblings spent many hours together because they lived near the generating station that their father oversaw, and away from towns or villages. Other families who worked with Arnim were their only other companions. As a result they were a marvellously close 'team'.

These cousins were a little older than we were and we felt a great deal of hero worship when we were fortunate enough to be in their company.

Their next move was to Ragged Rapids, near Bala, Ontario. At that time Uncle Arnim was in charge of a generating station for the Hydro so they lived about seven miles from Bala where the Hydro had four or five houses for the operators because someone was needed there around the clock. As the Second Great War became part of our existence, security was essential at the power plants around the country so one had to have clearance to visit.

Many hours were spent skating on pristine lakes during the frozen winter months, and they enjoyed hockey games at nearby Bala arena. During other seasons they swam, canoed and holidayed with family members in Cannington, Midland and Muskoka. Summers included staying at nearby Wasaga Beach where the sweeping golden beaches stretched forever. This is now a major tourist spot. The sandy beach runs for miles and tourists now vie for a spot in the sun. Many visits were made to Hamilton, too, as some of the other Taylor sisters had settled there.

Later, when High School dances in Gravenhurst were on the agenda, Arnim and Emily regularly sat through two sittings of whatever movie was on tap at the local theatre so the kids could enjoy the fun with their peers.

Norman Ambrose, our father, followed his brother Arnim. We will elaborate on his life in subsequent chapters, as he and Mary, our parents, are the main focus of these selected stories. Suffice it to say that at this time in his life he was frustrated that he could not join the army as his older brothers had done.

However, the forests in Western Canada were feeling the loss of young men to work in the backwoods in the forest industry.

So Norman answered the call to "Go West, young man. Go West." His ultimate destination was Weyburn, Saskatchewan.

Getting there was half the fun for adventurous young men. Fearlessly, they hopped aboard trains and empty boxcars, likely as ticket-less passengers and off they went to see the world.

Norm as a teenager

As many forestry workers were off to war, work was readily available and into the dense forests they went to take their chances. Norman recounted some rather hair raising tales of difficult living conditions, frosty dwelling, likely little more than hastily built shelters, and communal eating around the fire when possible.

Sometimes he drove the horses as they dragged logs through the woods but once he was detailed to assist the cook who had a dreadful temper. His last day there became quite terrifying as the cook became belligerent, wielded a huge, sharp knife in anger, and looked like he was ready to scalp someone. Norm didn't want it to be him! At once the decision was made that his days as a woodsman had come to an end, and off he ran at a gallop and headed for home. Merry chuckles always accompanied the retelling of this story as a wonderful glint shone in our father's eye.

He told of catching the train to Waubaushene and from there walked the frigid miles to their home. By the time he finally arrived home he was a mound of snow and ice and was quite a strange apparition. A young man's wonderful memories! We will leave him there for the time being and continue with the other children in the family.

Merton Linwood was only two years younger than Norm but it must have seemed to him that all of his bigger brothers had much more fun than he had. He had to stay at home on the farm and do all of those uninteresting chores while his brothers got to see the world and do marvellous things. He was a very quiet man all of his life. Perhaps he just couldn't get a word in edgewise with his siblings and their much more exciting stories.

Merton, or Mert as he was called, was an eligible bachelor for some time, and boarded with Norm and Mary in the early thirties when he first went to Uxbridge to work on the Hydro under Norm's leadership. Quiet though he was, he could tap dance like a pro, and delighted in whistling out a tune on his harmonica. That activity was always lively applauded by anyone within hearing.

For a while he seemed charmed by Mary's young sister Jean,who was working in Toronto but often visited Mary and Norm in Uxbridge. Mert and Jean enjoyed each other's company but parted ways. Jean liked her life in Toronto and was keen to stay there as a city girl.

Mert and his dog

Finally, Margaret Ferrier, a lovely young woman, caught his eye, and Mert became her proud husband. Marg lived with her family in nearby Sandy Hook but worked in Uxbridge.

After they married on 2 September 1940 Mert and Marg continued to live in Uxbridge where Mert worked with the Hydro. Soon they began buying property, making wonderful renovations, and then selling them for profit and moving on to the next task. Aunt Marg was tireless and seemed to have a knack for this kind of thing. Sisters-in-laws Mary and Marg could often be seen examining selections of wallpaper and materials for those newly appointed houses, which were truly attractive and which they sold very profitably. Aunt Marg had a wonderful laugh, was always cheerful and was a shrewd business partner for Mert. They're team work clicked and they continued to thrive. They also became the parents of Maribeth in 1946 and Lawrence Linwood (Larry), in 1949, which delighted everyone. I loved being the children's proud babysitter and taking them out in their prams and strollers.

Mert left the Hydro and next they moved to Manchester where they invested time and energy in a garage and snack bar. Again they met with success so the next move was to purchase Meadow Spring Lodge near Bobcagon. This became their delightful home and business from then on. New cottages and recreational facilities were added and it a great place for their children and for family celebrations as well.

When **Orin George**, the sixth son was born to Sherman and Essie he must have wondered why he had all of those tall brothers to look up to. Sometimes it was pretty foreboding, like the time Norm arrived home from his sojourn in the West in time for New Years celebrations. Orin was too young to remember him so was taken aback when Norm bounded into their home with happy cries. He was totally covered in snow and festooned with a ragged, snow-encrusted beard. Young Orin saw this huge white ghost and was completely terrified. This sent him rushing to hide in his mother's skirts in tears. Much coaxing was necessary before he was convinced that this was really just another of his big brothers.

Orin Belfry

It is quite understandable that Orin was lonely on the farm. The other boys had each other with whom to interact but Orin was just a little boy alone. Being thoughtful parents, Sherman and Essie decided that he needed a companion, so they adopted Dorothy from a Coldwater family known to friends, who were finding that another child was too much for them to look after. What a joy it was to have a close sibling, and truth to tell, perhaps having a little girl again was what Essie really wanted. Dorothy and Orin were inseparable as they grew up together. Her original family remained in contact and visits back and forth were continued.

Dorothy grew to be a beautiful young woman. She had golden curls, peaches and cream complexion and a sweet disposition. Unfortunately she was not strong and developed tuberculosis when she was in her mid-20s. This disease was not uncommon at the time, but it was very heartbreaking to have to take her to the sanatorium in Gravenhurst on Easter Sunday, 1938. The family loved her very much and visited her often. We children sat below her window and waved up at her while our parents visited. To us, she was like a fairy-tale princess in her ivory tower, but no doubt she felt as captive as those princesses of old.

Dorothy Belfry as a child

She later married Fred Rumney from the Vasey area. They were childless and continued to live in the area. Her health was never strong and she died in 1946 while still a young woman. Orin was particularly distraught to lose his wonderful companion.

The Belfrys get-together

Before an Orangemen's parade with Grandpa Belfry
<u>Back row:</u> Mel, Arnim, Grandpa Belfry, Norm
<u>Front row:</u> Gloria, Aunt Olive, Aunt Emily holding June, Ronnie, Marjorie and Aunt Dorothy

<u>Back row</u>: Orin, Mother Belfry, Olive, Mert, Norm and Mel holding Lee
<u>Front Row</u>: Ronnie, Doris, Father Belfry, and Margie (running)

Mary and Norm

In the summer and early fall before Mary and Norm were wed there were many preparations to make before the day they had looked forward to for so long. First there was the marriage of her sister Beatrice to Oliver Harrison. Their celebration took place in June of 1928, then the busy summer of gardens, thrashing, canning and trousseau gathering came next on the agenda. Mary had to have her tonsils removed too and that was an uncomfortable experience. Several school boards who heard that she had left her teaching position at Berkley called to try to lure her to their schools but that was not to be.

She and Norm made many plans. They proudly bought dining-room and bedroom furniture for their new home. Their upcoming move into a rented bungalow in the Toronto area was and exciting prospect. They were especially thrilled with the purchase of their pretty Limoges dishes which would be perfect on the oval walnut dining table and special trousseau linens. That set for twelve, although used regularly over the years, never suffered a crack. Mind you, we all were very careful of it as it was used for dinner every Sunday after church.

Now all was in readiness and the day of their wedding was nigh. After such a long delay they both were anxious for the rest of their lives to begin. Mary's diaries and scrapbooks will tell us about their beautiful wedding day and their new home.

Their wedding on November 13 1928 seems like a good place to begin this part of their story. They had originally planned to be married on the 12th but dear friend, Mabelle (Mabe) Parslow from Normal School who was always up to mischief, dared them to choose 'unlucky 13th' as their date. And so they did! Mary later was often heard to say that the 13 was a lucky number for them all of their lives.

Their marriage was solemnized at the Hillis homestead with Rev. Dr. Morrow officiating and Mrs. Morrow playing the wedding music. *The Hanover Post* tells us that:

Evergreens and pink and white streamers formed an arch beneath which the bridal party took their places. The bride was lovely in a frock of white georgette with white kid shoes and hosiery of a matching shade. Her flowers were pink sweet peas, roses and valley lilies and she wore the groom's gift, a wristwatch set with white sapphires.

That wristwatch is still beautiful and is treasured.

Mary and Norm, November 13, 1928

Following the ceremony a wedding dinner was served. The bride's table was centred with a beautiful wedding cake and decorated in pink and white in keeping with the artistic decorations elsewhere in the home.

Later in the afternoon the newlyweds left on a motor trip to Midland, Cannington, Victoria Harbour and other points. The bride donned a smart brown ensemble with chic hat and accessories to harmonize. On their return they will take up residence in Toronto.

Mary and Norm first home was in Etobicoke; they moved to two more homes in Islington during the next two years. Mary did some supply teaching and she loved to tell about the interview she had in order to be employed there.

It seems that she had heard that the man in charge of hiring was quite a hard taskmaster, so she resolved to wear her most sedate outfit should she be called for an interview. To her chagrin one day, she went to answer the door and came face to face with the gentleman in question. And she remembered what she was wearing, a very, very short flapper dress!

"Oh, no!" she thought. "I probably won't get the job". However, he must have been suitably impressed because she did indeed get the job and enjoyed the opportunity to do what she loved so much. During the time they were there she enjoyed her teaching assignments in Eatonville School and Islington Public School.

In thinking about this prospective employer arriving unannounced at her home, it seems like a rather unusual thing to do, at least from our perspective. However, he undoubtedly learned a great deal about her from his call, how she kept her home, as well as how well she could conduct herself on the spur of the moment. Not many of us would consider this appropriate business practice now.

They also had some boarders who were taking courses with Norm, and needed a place to sleep during the weekdays. She was only required to supply the bedrooms and did not have to feed them so it seemed like a good idea. Norm was on a training course with the Hydro and these men were as well. One night shortly after their wedding a number of their friends and relatives in the city had a lovely shower for them with nearly three-dozen guests attending.

The evening included presents, laughter, good food and lots of fun. On returning home they found that there had been an uninvited visit to their bedroom and everything had been turned topsy-turvy. And she was horrified that the word "**Visitors!?!**" had been scrawled in big black letters in her precious diary. Perhaps this was a form of shivaree where friends would make unannounced calls on newlyweds but I did think it was rather rude to write in something as personal as her diary.

And as the decade was coming to an end, she and Norman were very happy and very much in love.

But the economic state of the country was soon to be shaken by the Great Crash of 29 October 1929. Banks became bankrupt, financial institutions collapsed and many folks lost their money, their investments, their jobs and in some cases their lives. This heralded the Great Depression but as yet this couple were not investors and would not fully appreciate how the world would be affected by this social and economic disaster.

The Thirties and Forties

Norman's training with the Hydro was completed in March of 1930 and he was sent to Uxbridge, a small town near Toronto to form a new area for Ontario Hydro. This was a very new experience, and a real challenge. He had only worked for Ontario Hydro for ten years, most of which was as a lineman climbing poles and installing transformers, cables and wires. He had had no experience in offices or as a salesperson. He had taken several correspondence courses in English and mathematics to help round out some of the things he'd missed out on as a boy, but he'd had no management training except for the crash course given by the Hydro while they were in Etobicoke.

In those years one had to 'sell hydro' to the farmers, not the easiest thing to do in the midst of the Depression. Money was scarce and farmers were fearful about signing up for this new commodity. Good salesmanship was definitely required. It is also true that people's attitude played an important role in this process. If one farmer put his name on the line and agreed to this new plan, his neighbours, not waning to be out done, would also sign and soon, enough farmers agreed so that the work was able begin.

Inexperienced men from the surrounding community were hired, office space was rented, lines were staked out and men started the backbreaking job of laying down the lines. Men dug, dug, dug, then raised poles, strung wires, installed meters and before long became seasoned, experienced men who took great pride in doing the work of bringing power to the local area. It was a thrilling experience for both farmers and workmen when "the hydro" was finally turned on.

Many of those men became Norm's lifelong friends so his skill with people must have been considerable.

This new position required much planning and good common sense, and Norman was a natural, much like his brother Roy in nearby Cannington. Visits back and forth always included some 'shop talk' as these two brothers shared their similar positions and concerns.

During those first years the office phone was connected to the Belfry phone so Norm could take calls when the office was closed. Later, as we grew up we took turns manning the phone during a storm, candles at the ready. Many of the area farmers had gradually turned to poultry farming and it was always critical that heat and power was on when the chicks were in the incubation stage. Where ever possible Norm contacted those whose business required power if he knew that there would be interruptions. Frequent phone calls during power outages were often required. His thoughtful approach helped to cement his reputation as a committed, caring leader.

When they moved to Uxbridge, Mary often went along on trouble calls, to hold a spotlight so Norm could make the required adjustments, or just keep him company. Their teamwork was a constant source of pleasure and they did love being together.

The Depression that began in 1929 forced many men out of work, and resulted in homelessness and unemployment. Many prowled the countryside, looking for work, for a meal, or an extra sweater to keep from freezing in someone's barn. Often they slept in the local police cell if one was available.

The first house Mary and Norm rented in Uxbridge was just on the edge of town and many, many destitute travellers knocked on their door.

Mary was compassionate, and regularly asked them to step in so she could give them a meal. She remembered one particular gentleman who spoke in cultured tones and who was dreadfully embarrassed to ask for a bit of food. As was her habit, she set a place for him at her prized dining room table, and served him some bacon and eggs. On returning to the kitchen for milk, toast and jam, her curiosity was piqued and she glanced through the door jamb to see what he was doing. How awful! She saw him frantically pushing the food into his mouth with both hands. Before she returned she made certain that he could hear her coming and not be too embarrassed. Again he was the epitome of decorum and used perfect manners.

Mary never forgot the humiliation that she had witnessed through the door. One of the gentlemen whom she helped told her that it was common knowledge among the transients that a good meal and assistance was always available in their home at the edge of town. Those early years left a mark on her even though they were never without food and shelter themselves. She felt that having good food was a privilege, and it was not to be wasted in her home. It was impressed upon us children not to ask for more if food remained on our plates. It was a good lesson for all of us.

In thinking about this happening, one wonders at the wisdom of asking strangers into one's home. It was clear that she was there alone. She was never to regret her kindness and compassion to those who called at her door. Perhaps the need for food was so strong that none of her unexpected visitors took advantage of the situation. The frequent robberies and violence we read about in today's world were unheard of then. Surprising how times and circumstances change the mores of the day.

The ramifications of the stock market crash were to reverberate in increasing circles for a very long time. Banks foreclosed, many businesses and individuals faced bankruptcy and wealthy bankers, company presidents and political figures sometimes chose suicide as the only acceptable avenue open to them. The economy and the social structures of the country would take a long time to settle down.

More moves seemed necessary. People who happily rented homes to Mary and Norm seemed to find that they needed to help relatives out soon after Mary and Norm had painted and redecorated. After all the work of cleaning, painting and fixing things up nicely this young couple too often would discover that a needy relative would be moving in almost immediately. One large house was in dreadful shape with plaster and paint literally falling off the walls. What a mess! Their landlords did agree that everything needed refurbishing. It was backbreaking work and some of them did help Mary on occasion. The hours of dust, and confusion made for very poor quality of life, but a lovely home finally emerged.

Then, when finished and beautiful, an urgent need by a 'relative' soon necessitated another move. Suspicious? Of course, no leases were given so hands were tied. But this last rental experience convinced them they must buy their own home. And so they contracted to have a new bungalow built in a central part of town.

Not only had they been busy redecorating homes, they had had a long awaited addition their family. To their wonder, a son, Ronald Keith, was born on 4 April 1932. Mary had been having some rather severe health problems and had been paralysed so was rushed to St Michael's Hospital 40 miles away in Toronto.

The roads were slick with ice and it was a frightening drive. It was also too soon for their baby but Ronnie thought the time was right to make his appearance so arrived as a four and a half pound beautiful little boy. They were thrilled! He was very fragile, developed double pneumonia and was in an incubator for the first weeks of his life and Mary was unable even to hold him for quite a while.

Norm was kept busy going back and forth from Uxbridge to Toronto to see them, and he was obliged to secure a bank loan to cover the $650 needed for hospital bills, a staggering sum to be sure. These could not have been easy times. Medical insurance was still only a dream and likely many others found themselves in the same dilemma.

Mary's sister Jean and Aunt Ella were frequent and most welcome visitors for Mary and the baby during their Toronto stay. Eventually Mary was strong enough to look after Ronnie and his needs, and some weeks later they were indeed thrilled when they could take him home to Uxbridge.

He was not strong and needed a great deal of care for the next few years of his life. But he was precious and they felt like the luckiest people in the world. Fortunately for all of them Ronnie slept a good bit of the time, giving welcome opportunities for Mary and Norm to catch their breath and regain their strength.

The home they were living in at that time was right across from the High School and to everyone's surprise another tiny baby, also premature, arrived a year and a half later. That baby was me, and I too decided to join the family before I had grown very big. And I was insistent so there was no chance of going to Toronto, and no hospital in Uxbridge.

Mary had a long and difficult birth and the two doctors who attended her in her home were working without much equipment. A great deal of ether was used during the lengthy ordeal, perhaps almost too much. Quite likely that is why I arrived as a blue baby and very reluctant to breathe. Mary heard the older doctor whisper to his colleague that they would "try to save the mother but there was not much hope for the kid!"

How difficult this must have been for her to hear. Fortunately the younger doctor had other ideas. He tried to shock my heart by placing me first under a hot faucet, followed quickly by a dunking in cold water. The hoped for improvement did not occur. When that didn't start me breathing he used adrenaline hypos directly into the heart to shock it into action. It worked! This was certainly not standard treatment, but thanks to his recent training and his medical expertise he made the right choice and I decided that I might just like this place after all. The day was October 3rd 1933 and I was four pounds eight ounces and named Margaret Esther after my two grandmothers, Margaret Hillis and Esther Belfry.

It is interesting that years later when our own children were taking allergy shots, our paediatrician gave me a prescription for adrenaline serum to keep on hand in case they had an adverse reaction to their allergy medication that he had recently taught me how to administer. So, Dr. Smith was certainly well ahead of his time.

As the old saying goes, having a son and a daughter is a millionaire's family. Mary and Norm thought so too. They might have had some quiet doubts though as I slept quite well during the day, but from ten at night till three in the morning I chose to exercise my vocal chords very lustily. This happened not once in a while, but every night for three months. The joys of new parenthood! Dr. Smith, the young doctor and his wife came for dinner and the evening one night during that time, and he was shocked when he heard me howl.

Mary had told him about this nightly serenade but he didn't believe that anything that small could create such a continuous uproar. Isn't it wonderful that some of our most uncomfortable happenings fade into almost forgotten memories over the years! My parents never held it against me, but I'm sure they had some very exhausted times during my howling escapades.

The next couple of years must have been busy ones. Mary's diaries are full of details of our first sentences, a few minor falls, new teeth and lots of visiting with friends and family. It was a happy young family who took pleasure in each other. Mary's beloved mother died in 1930 and she still missed her very much. New neighbours and friends began to fill the void that was created by losing one's parents. Many of these friends stayed in very close touch for many, many years.

Mary and her sisters were very troubled when news from home told them that their father had married again in 1931. His new wife, Florence Mary Henry of Brampton, had come as a housekeeper but as it was unseemly for a couple to share the same house without marriage, a convenient ceremony was performed.

This marriage ended with her death in 1939 after which our Grandfather was married again to Jessie Marshall who was quite a bit younger than he was. Again the sisters were concerned but they were encouraged to visit and reestablish family connections. Jessie remained with Wilson until his death in the 1950s.

Gradually they felt more welcome in the family home and our holiday visits were resumed. The sisters did love to get together and our families enjoyed getting to know cousins.

Uxbridge was a growing community and as the town grew so did local associations. Both Mary and Norm were active in a number of things; Trinity United Church, I.O.D.E. (Imperial Order of the Daughters of the Empire) for Mary and Masonic Lodge and a new arena for hockey filled the hours for Norm. There were also many delightful evenings spent with friends playing bridge or just enjoying each other' company and busy days watching their children grow.

During the next few years Mary had a number of health concerns. Impacted wisdom teeth caused much pain and even long after they were extracted the poison in her body caused arthritis problems. She had several operations; for appendicitis, cystic ovaries and displaced uterus. She was very anemic and needed painful iron shots to bolster her system as well so we required home help. We particularly remember one lady whom my brother and I dubbed 'Squash face'. Not a nice thing to do but we were young (and we only said it softly to ourselves).

Norm was busy building up his Hydro area and it was thriving. He and Roy often got together for meetings and to share knowledge and information about their jobs.

Mary took up snowshoeing with some of her lady friends and she knitted, and kept very active.

In the late 1930"s Sherman and Essie moved into a stone home in the village of Victoria Harbour on the shores of Georgian Bay. There members of the family gathered for birthdays, Christmas and other occasions.

It was very exciting to visit there and we remember peering out the car window oh so carefully to see who would be the first one to spot Grandma's Lake. And what a happy group it was when we were all there. The sons and daughters had grown into affectionate families and continued the family penchant for keeping in touch. They often visited back and forth in each other's homes during the year, and took many joint family holidays, such as camping in the Ontario northland

The Sherman Belfry home in Victoria Harbour

As families and fortune allowed, the siblings began renting adjoining cottages in Haliburton where all ages could relax together.

Linus, Mark and Laura Vasey, Ron, Marg and Norm Belfry at Parry Sound Reforestation Lookout

Our Grandparent's Victoria Harbour home was near the bay so our winter fun included skating on the frozen expanse of ice. Our parents were quick to check that the space was safe enough for our swirls and fun before we ventured out.

Many family trips were made to see the senior Belfrys when the women would do the housecleaning and leave copious trays of baking. All the wives were enthusiastic cooks and could produce tarts, cakes, pies, and cookies in a flash. The table was always laden. As children we loved those excursions. During the drive to our grandparent's home Mother would give us each a handful of raisins and ask us to see who could chew each one thirty times. I expect those were presented to us about the time we became restless in the back seat.

In January 1936 the country mourned the death of King George V of England whose son Edward VIII came to the British throne as king. This was followed by great concerns because Edward, rather a party type, had fallen in love with a twice divorced American woman named Wallis Simpson. Everyone feared that he would marry her, but the Church of England was adamant that such behaviour was forbidden for their king. While collective breaths were held, Edward struggled with his dilemma.

Finally on 10 December 1936 he broadcasted his plan to the nation. He had decided to renounce his role as king to marry his love. I suspect there was sadness coupled with collective sighs of relief around the globe at this decision. This meant that King George VI, his brother would succeed as the next king.

Mary's comments in her diary at the end of this year were: *This old year of 1936 has seen three kings; King George V died in January, King Edward VIII gave up the throne for the love of a woman in December and his brother, King George VI, took the throne instead. We lived in two homes this year.*

George, a gentle man who sometimes stuttered when he talked, his gracious wife Queen Elizabeth, and their two children, Elizabeth, our present queen, and her sister, Margaret Rose, became the royal family. Queen Elizabeth, later to be called Queen Mum, was patient and caring and worked with King George so that he overcame his shyness and his speech problems. She was a gracious monarch and was beloved by the whole realm until her death in the early part of the 21st century. Their years at the helm were good years and they endeared themselves to people throughout the world.

Mary's beloved sister, Jean, who had been Dr. Ogden's receptionist in Toronto, became the beautiful bride of Charles Fursman on 4 June 1938 in Oakville United Church, Toronto. The Fursman farm where Charles grew up was not far from the Hillis farm outside of Hanover and the families had known each other for some time.

After their wedding they moved to a lovely large home on Ellerbeck Avenue.in Toronto and lived there for many years. Charles was in the haberdashery business and Jean kept housekeeping rooms in their large house which had been a part of the Playter Estates in Toronto's heyday. They did not have children.

Jean Hillis and Charles Fursman, June 1938

While Mary and Norm were busily coping with the business of being parents, they kept in close touch with the other siblings, who were also having children and/or managing careers. They were happily involved in the growth of this community, but always ready for company or fun.

The new house was taking shape and nearly ready for occupancy but this is when the big house in the north end of town which they had so recently remodelled became no longer available to them. It seemed there were needy relatives again. Accommodation was scarce and the only place left to go until their home was ready was an apartment over an ice cream parlour on the main street of town. There were many steps up, and with two young children, anything but suitable, but it was the only choice. So move they did.

As luck would have it Mary became very ill and again went to Toronto for surgery. It is hard to imagine how they juggled things and kept going, but somehow they did. Just like the farming communities of old, this close knit community helped with casseroles, babysitting, moral support and whatever was needed so the days and weeks ticked by. Likely knowing that they would soon be in their own home must have kept their spirits up.

Mary's diary mentions that *"The children had their first platform appearance at the Sunday school concert and did very well"*. Many more of those would happen over the years.

She also spoke of the joy of camping in Algonquin Park with Norm's parents and in other lovely sites with some of their Uxbridge friends. The men saw moose, deer and wolf tracks in the forest, and once caught 26 grand trout. What a tasty dinner that was. During one holiday they visited Calendar to see the Dionne Quintuplets, Canada's first. Crowds of tourists turned up daily to buy tickets to watch those five little girls playing in their sandboxes. The children were badly exploited and were never free of the unwanted spotlight that plagued their early lives. What unhappy lives they were to lead in the fishbowl of media attention.

Camping was what we loved to do best on our holidays and Twelve Mile Lake was a very favourite place to vacation. We'd sit on the edge of the backseat in the car, straining to see who could be first to glimpse the hotel called The Red Umbrella Inn. That meant that just around the corner was our best loved campsite. While our parents were busy setting up the tent, we'd scamper down to the beach to find the 'separator' we had left the year before. This was a huge piece of gnarled driftwood with all kinds of orifices and when we put cans or dishes under the openings we had our own milk separator just like our Grandfather Hillis. Our parents must have chuckled at the town kids wanting to be like just farm children.

The backseat of the car was a perfect fit for me so became my camp bed for the tent. I really tried to remember that it was NOT in the car when we went to the well for water, but sometimes I forgot. The sudden, surprise stop when I flopped down was a graphic reminder to be more careful.

Ron and Marg, Twelve Mile Lake

The next few years in their new home were busy gardening, landscaping, planting apple trees (mine was a Yellow Harvest and my brothers a Spy), and getting to know the neighbours. Our annual two week holiday camping trips took us to Horseshoe Lake and other beauty spots in Haliburton. Those holidays were so special. With the tent, the Coleman stove, some pots and our great black frying pan we were ready for anything. We thought that sitting around the campfire toasting marshmallows was just about the most exciting thing we could do.

Camping, Ron, Norm and Marg

Once when we were enjoying a campfire with our nearby campers, our dad pulled a flaming marshmallow to his lips to blow out the fire. Oops! Too close. The fire lit on his nose and gave him a dreadful burn. Being a quiet man, he slipped down to the water and put it out without comment. The next day his nose was fiery and red, and very, very sore. Everyone thought it was a great joke except him.

Mary and Norm often socialized with their many friends too and the decades rolled along as they should. Their group loved to get all decked out and go to the Royal York Hotel in Toronto for the dinner dances there. After a delightful dinner they would dance the night away to the strains of Stan St. John's excellent band. Stan was the brother of one of their Uxbridge friends and so it made for a very special evening. We loved to see our mother's long dresses and sparkling eyes as they set out for the city.

One historical highlight of that time was the train trip through the countryside that King George and Queen Elizabeth made in June of 1939. We watched the beautiful royal train from the station at Beaverton and did so want to see these royal people. Would they look like those in our story books? Finally King George, dressed just like our parents, came out on the platform at the back as the train was pulling out. Where was his crown? Aunt Lu raised her voice and cried, "We want the Queen!" and to our delight, out she came and graciously waved her hand to everyone. Her smile was beautiful and we were completely thrilled. Our day was complete.

Little did any of us realize that scant month later we would hear that Britain had declared war on Germany, and this meant that Canada was also involved. The news was on every radio and shock waves were felt all over the world. The world was forever changed that September Sunday afternoon in 1939. From then on families were glued to the nightly radio news reports that were served up with our evening meal. No one dared speak. It was an anxious time for everyone.

Uncle Orin was now eligible for service so, along with many other young men he quickly enlisted in the army. Poor Grandma and Grandpa Belfry once again had to face the anxiety of having a son march off to war. Although we were young, I well remember how sad we were as we watched him board the train in Uxbridge, heading for active duty. Aunt Marion, his wife, stayed with Mert and Marg in Uxbridge and worked in the Hydro office there.

This scene was re-enacted over and over during the next few years. We remember the day we were lined up outside our Public School in Uxbridge about to go in from recess. Then our beloved principal Mr. Stockford joined us to tell us that he was leaving for active duty the next day. Teachers and some older students had trouble keeping their composure during his caring farewell. Unfortunately he was not one of the lucky ones. He never came back to his homeland.

Those war years cast a gloom over the whole world. The commonwealth countries rallied, and soon young men became soldiers and rushed to aid the oppressed countries. Not only was most of Europe under siege, but in December of 1941 Japanese forces attacked Pearl Harbour so the United States quickly joined the war. Now the Pacific Front was added to the fray.

War news was the main topic of concern over the next few years. Many women at home spent weekly Red Cross sessions preparing bandages for the wounded. Many other women joined the work force and became shift workers in munitions factories beside the men who could not volunteer for service in the military because of age or health concerns. School children saved War Saving Stamps too. The whole countryside was galvanized into action. Letters and care packages were sent to service men, and many prayers were offered for their safety. Norman and the rest of the Area Managers refused pay raises for the duration of the war as their contribution. Everywhere else salaries were escalating so this was a generous act of solidarity which they supported until peace was declared.

Mary and Norm always enjoyed the annual Hydro Conventions held in Toronto. Aside from being a mini family get together, they loved meeting and mingling with others who were holding responsible positions in this company. They enjoyed the luxury of the Royal York, the fancy banquets and the women liked to shop while the men attended meetings.

One memorable winter their train became trapped as they travelled to the conference and it took four days instead of the usual hour or so to reach Toronto. A dreadful snowstorm had completely closed all of the tracks and they were captive. But all was not lost. A large farmhouse was near enough for them to get to by climbing over the snowbanks. There they found hot food and shelter. Mary made tea biscuits in the farmer's kitchen, someone else made soup and stew, and it turned into an exciting escapade. When they finally reached the Royal York on the Thursday the conference was over and everyone else was on the way home. How they loved to tell about the sing-songs, the camaraderie and the fun that was part of the snowbound experience.

One of the special celebrations that we shared as a family was the 50th Anniversary of our grandparents, Esther and Sherman Belfry. An Open House was to be held for friends and neighbours and the daughters-in-law sprung into action. They were all accomplished cooks and produced platters of tasty goodies for the many friends who came to wish the happy couple well. I can remember meeting this plan with a bit of anxiety as it was to be the first day in my three years at school that I would miss being in class. I was assured that it was a legitimate reason to be absent from school.

But a new green dress appeared and it was very pretty. There were to be some compensations, it seemed. We cousins were all fancied up and it was a wonderful time to be together. Many relatives appeared; Belfrys, Neys and Taylors and what fun it was to listen to them all enjoy exchange news and views. That always made a joyous occasion.

Here some of the grandkids take a break from the party to relax outdoors
Back row: Gar Vasey, Doris Belfry, Jerry Vasey
Front row: Nelda Vasey, Ron and Marg and Lee Belfry, Mark Vasey
Children of Laura, Mel and Norm

During those early years of the 1940s our father began having a great deal of trouble with his eyes. A visit to the optometrist became something of a worry because he was told he should see his doctor as soon as possible. Our physician was Dr. Lockwood in Cannington so Norm coupled his appointment with a visit to Roy and Lu, and Mary went along.

The news they heard that day was not good. Norm learned that he had a serious case of diabetes and would have to go on a very rigid diet. Dr. Lockwood felt that they could get things under control by being very careful about his food intake, so dieting was began thus avoiding daily insulin injections. Norm was a large man with a healthy appetite so this took serious determination.

Christmas of 1942 was only a few weeks after this diagnosis. Usually he savoured all the wonderful delicacies that went with the festive season, but this year they were not for him. The poultry stuffing, the sweet cranberries and the fancy pastries were absolutely taboo. Poor Norm decided that his best move would be to leave Grandma Belfry's groaning table so that he wouldn't be too tempted. While everyone else munched on traditional Christmas fare, Norm took his watery tasteless Junket dessert to the kitchen and quietly ate alone. It was tough but he kept to the diet. Slowly the pounds started to drop away.

Shortly after, when his resistance was quite low, he contracted streptococcus of the blood stream. This virulent infection was extremely hard to shake and penicillin was still to be discovered.

Before we knew it he was very ill. In a matter of weeks he became gaunt, exhausted, and lost a great deal of weight. There was no hospital in Uxbridge so he had to stay home and Mary became his 24-hour nurse. All of his dishes and linens had to be sterilized and his diet carefully monitored. In spite of the fact that he was living in his bedroom at home, we were unable to see him for nearly a month. We were young but realized the seriousness of his condition so tried to be helpful. A new drug called Sulfa was in use for war casualties so this was prescribed and it proved to be most effective. My brother and I were met each day with inquires about his progress. When he finally was able to join the family again he had lost 30 pounds and was a pale shadow of himself.

Slowly the long process of becoming well began. For a start a large apartment above the Hydro office was rented for us, and Dad was able to go downstairs to work on an irregular basis as his physical condition warranted. This lasted until he could finally begin a normal routine. Support from friends and business associates helped greatly to get him back on his feet. It was a time when individuals were treated as valuable assets of a company, and taken care of by their employers.

One of Uncle Roy's friends had a large house trailer so offered its use to us for a month of rest and relaxation at nearby Lake Simcoe. What a wonderful gesture that was. That summer was a special healing time for all of us. The cares of the world were put aside and Dad spent hours canoeing on the bay or resting in the sun. Just what the doctor ordered for both Mary and Norm. It was a summer devoted to regaining his health and was marvellous for us as a family.

Foods were rationed and one needed stamps for such commodities as butter and sugar. Mary was perfecting the fine art of canning fruits and vegetables with a water-packing method so we not particularly inconvenienced by the shortages.

Norm at his favourite pastime

As a consequence we did not have sweet desserts very often and all were healthier for this. Dad's health improved and gradually he was able to resume his involvement in the Masonic Lodge, the Area School Board representative and curling.

War news was terrible with dreadful reports of atrocities, death camps, prisoners of war, destruction of historical landmarks, and devastated cities. Bombs and air raids became everyday occurrences in many major locations, but the tide did eventually turn. For a while our cousin Jack Hudson was a prisoner of war and this was cause for great anxiety, as it was for all who had relatives missing or imprisoned.

Finally in May of 1945 a truce was called in the European theatre of war. Bells rang out all over the world. At school we all filed out of our classrooms and marched outside to wave our arms and cheer. Brother Ron took it one step farther and rang the big school bell, a fact that did not please the School principal. Afterwards we wondered where his sense of patriotism was that day. It did seem like a poor approach to such a happy event.

Parades took place all over the world and crowds laughed, cheered, and gave thanks. The spontaneous parade down Uxbridge Main Street was one we shall all remember.

Slowly soldiers, sailors and airmen came home, some badly scarred, some with shattered limbs and many happily with brides they had met, fallen in love with, and married.

We were thrilled when Mary's nephew Jack Hudson, sister Florence's son, brought Peggy Pentland, a lovely Scottish wife, home to our family after their September 1945 wedding.

Then in July the atomic bomb was dropped on Hiroshima, causing horror and destruction. This last atrocity was the catalyst to bring the war to its final conclusion. People resumed their prewar jobs again to some extent but many changes could be seen in the work place, and indeed in the social fibre of post war life. Many women did not relish going back to a quiet home and there was much needed restructuring of the roles of people in society.

Soldiers were going back to schools and universities with government assistance and great shifts in thinking were creating a newer, more modern society. And life was either settling down or getting more involved depending on the various ages and stages of the players.

And what had been happening to the members of the Belfry family?

During the 1930s Aunt Laura and Uncle Linus had moved to Toronto with their four children. It was lovely having them closer and we visited back and forth regularly.

Our family often had a 'children's day' when we went to the Toronto for shoes, clothing and household needs, saw a movie and visited Mary's sister Jean who was married and lived there on Ellerbeck Avenue near the Danforth, or Norm's sister Laura and family who lived across from Christie Pits.

Sometimes we went to a fancy restaurant too and my brother and I loved that part. We felt especially grown-up one day when both of our parents had had eye appointments which necessitated eye drops for the exam. Trouble started when we went to the restaurant for lunch a few minutes later. Both of them soon realized that they couldn't see to read the menu. How special we felt as we told them what the daily blue plate would include.

Another day as Dad and I walked along Queen Street. to meet the rest of the family, Dad heard an odd sound as his feet hit the pavement. He looked down to see what was wrong and saw that one of his toe rubbers had been lost. Without breaking stride he stepped to the side of the curb, slipped off the one remaining toe rubber, and continued along the street without a comment. What a good laugh we had at Dad's expense as we returned to the car late in the day and saw the 'other rubber' quietly waiting on the floor of the car where Dad had been sitting.

Uncle Mel and Aunt Olive were leading busy lives, too, as hydro requirements and growing families kept them on the hop. But they were never too busy to take part in family vacations. They especially enjoyed camping at Wasaga Beach on Georgian Bay with brother Arnim and his family. The beach at that time was a long wonderful expanse of golden sand and a popular place to congregate and/or use for car races along the glistening stretch. Certainly none of those beauty spots had yet been dedicated to the beautiful Provincial Parks that we see now. But the sand was fabulous and there was plenty of room to play.

Cousins at Victoria Harbour:
Back row, Gloria and Donald (Bala)
Front row Marg and Ron (Uxbridge), Lee and Doris (Markdale).

I felt very important to be invited to visit with the Markdale Belfrys for two weeks in the early 1940s. Spending time with Doris and Leona was like having older sisters. What fun!!

While there I remember Uncle Mel daring me to sit in a high chair that had been used by a visitor, AND to get out without lifting the tray. It seemed like no problem and I readily took the bet. Then I tried to extricate myself and the fun began.

Oh how I tried, but the catcalls and general hilarity did me in until I finally had to cry, "UNCLE!" Uncle Mel threw back his head and howled with laughter. Me, I was totally embarrassed.

For the second week we went to Loon Lake in Muskoka where we were to meet Roy and Lu. Lee and Doris remember that we met our uncle and aunt en route and they were amazed that Lu and Roy's car looked as if they'd taken a shovel to pack it with everything just heaved into the back seat. Aunt Lu, who was quite a fascinating individual, had broken ribs at the time and was wearing Uncle Roy's long winter underwear. What a sight she was. Naturally the three of us snickered behind our palms at her attire.

Her surprising antics are remembered with glee. She insisted on using my new popcorn popper (which I had purchased to take home as a gift for my parents!) to catch little frogs for bait, and after yelling for someone to help keep her frog on her fishing line, when out trolling for a catch. Later on our way back to shore, she regaled the whole lake by singing, "*Pull for the shore, sailors, pull for the shore*" as loud as her lungs would allow. Music to row by, I guess.

She generally kept us in stitches with songs, card games and silly sayings so holidays when she was around were never dull. It was a great holiday and the first one I had spent two weeks away from my parents so at almost nine I felt quite grown-up. Perhaps I had just realized that there was a whole world out there to explore and it could be a pretty interesting thing to do.

Our Cousins

There were many more opportunities over the years to get together with our Belfry cousins. Often Victoria Harbour was the meeting place as we all visited our grandparents. It was great to check each other's height to see how we were all growing.

Jerald, Laura and Linus' oldest son, married Pauline Tucker in 1947 at the Vasey home in Toronto. Jerry and Pauline met at Essex Street School in Grade Seven, and Pauline remembers that they both really loved Country music. One of their favourite things to do on a date was to go dancing at the Palais Royal down at Sunnyside. This popular entertainment spot drew people from all over the city like a magnet for many years.

Jerry and Pauline, Horseshow Lake, 1947

Jerald also became a Hydro Employee, serving in the forestry department for nearly 39 years. On retirement he and Pauline very much enjoyed spending time travelling the highways and byways of Canada, as well as visiting their children and watching their grand-children grow.

Jerry and Pauline had four children, Roy, Nelda, Janet, and Jill, and later eight grandchildren whom Jerry loved to spoil. We again see that family names reoccur. Young Roy was named after Roy, Jerry's uncle and their daughter Nelda was named after his sister. Pauline says that Jerry was a man of few words but his word was his bond, just like that of his own dad's. 'He was honest, trustworthy, a wonderful dad and super husband who lived his life by the Golden

Rule'. What a lovely tribute to a life partner. Pauline now lives in Hamilton and misses Jerry, who died in 1989.

Linus and Laura's second son was Garnet, a big, blond bombshell in the hockey arena. His ability and energy made him a standout. He played successfully in the American Hockey League and then headed to Scotland to help introduce the game of hockey to that bonny isle. He was very handsome, too, and became quite a hit with the local young women of Ayre where he lived. Among the teams for whom he was a star are the Dunfurmaline Vikings, the Ayre Raiders and the Glasgow Bruins. Later he also was a playing coach in both England and Italy. I remember reading press releases from that time when he was photographed surrounded by a bevy of adoring fans. His fair colouring and arresting good looks caused quite a stir. Gar as he was called, married the red-haired Scottish lass named Peggy whom he met in Brighton before returning to Canada, and they now live in southern Ontario.

Mark, the third son, and my brother Ron were close in age and visited back and forth. In the 1950s as a young single teacher in Toronto, I often met Mark when out for the evening and he, the perfect gentleman, was quick to offer a drive home if needed. I was a regular visitor at Aunt Laura's home so we frequently were in touch. One visit was especially delightful when I met Berryl, whom Mark was to marry shortly. They married around 1958 and he and Berryl had several children, eventually separated and Mark, who worked for the Hydro for 27 years, died in 1978 from cancer.

Nelda, the fourth child and only daughter in the family and I were close in age and kept in touch regularly for some years. Once when she was quite young she ate an enormous meal at our home, after which she declared, "I'm so full my legs are stiff!" That became a classic saying in our house when we were really stuffed.

When we were in our mid-teens we spent parts of many holidays visiting each other. Nelda usually spent part of the Christmas holidays with us and I often went to visit her during the Easter vacation. We got to know each other's friends and felt most comfortable in each other's homes. Was that where I learned to enjoy city living I wonder? There was so much to do and see there and we usually packed the time together with as much activity as possible. At that time they lived across from Christie Pits, now called Christie Park I believe, so there was what seemed like continuous entertainment. Sports, company, activity -- amazing choices for a small town girl.

A highlight of one spring vacation was the morning Nelda and I hurried downtown to the Casino, a well known movie theatre on Queen Street West. We were prepared for a long wait to get tickets because the red hot crooner, Johnny Rae, was there in person and we wanted to hear him sing his #1 hit 'Cry'. Slowly we snaked along the street to the west, then turned the corner onto Queen St. There were still many people in line before us, and we were quite anxious that tickets would still be available. Finally we reached the box office. Yes, there still tickets. Ah, the thrill!! Johnny brought the house down with his sobbing renditions of 'Cry' and 'The Little White Cloud That Cried' while swaying with the mike. Our feet hardly touched ground on our return home. My small town was never that exciting.

In 1955 Nelda married Phil Chapman, born about 1931, whom she met in 1953 in High School. Phil was a keen athlete and played hockey. He was a team member of the Toronto Marlies and the Oshawa Generals in his younger years. Nelda and Phil had four children; Michael, 1956, who married Debbie and had 4 children, Carol, 1959, who married Danny and had 2 children, Cindy, 1960, who married Ken and had one child, and Paul, 1962, who married Rose had 5 children.

Nelda and Phil love to travel and have taken many world cruises. After 50+ years they still are very much in love and enjoy golf, reading, swimming, and frequent visits to Florida.

And now is a good time to see how Gloria and the other Bala Belfrys were getting along. Arnim's children were reaching adulthood and Gloria, the eldest was the next of our cousins to consider leaving home. Toronto was her choice and there she trained as a nurse at Sick Children's Hospital. On graduation in 1947 she nursed at Sick Kids for a year then moved to Kenora where her friend from training was living. Following that she did private duty nursing in Hamilton where a number of the Taylor family lived. While in Hamilton she met Bob Arkinson. Sparks flew and thirteen weeks later Bob and Gloria were married on Sept 9 1949 and moved to Bob's hometown, Montreal. They moved back to Niagara Falls in 1951 and soon Bob became another of the family to join the Hydro where he remained until retirement.

Bob and Gloria in Florida

June, Gloria's youngest sister, had finished her teacher training in Toronto and was happily teaching in an inner city school in the heart of the city. I was just starting my own teacher training in Toronto at that time so June and I were able to get together every so often to spend part of a weekend catching up on family and each other.

Once when our fathers were in Toronto for the annual convention they had a neat surprise for us. Would we like to go out for dinner and then see Mel Tormé, 'The Velvet Fog' in a performance at the Casino? By all means, we would love it and thought they were a pretty great pair of fathers for suggesting it. It was a great evening, and we were thrilled to be squired by two such handsome gentlemen.

June Belfry Rodell

Around that time air travel was beginning to be a possibility for ordinary folk and the airlines were starting to look for dynamic, versatile stewardesses, so on a lark June applied. To her surprise she was hired and soon went into their training program. Before she knew it she was winging her way to New York as a beautiful stewardess for American Airlines.

While on duty one day she and her friend, wearing their stewardess uniforms, were canvassing for a charitable association in Manhattan.

Along came Herb Rodell, a representitive for Burlington Mills. Herb couldn't stop thinking about the lovely brunette so, not knowing which one had intrigued him, he called the airlines and asked questions until he discovered which stewardesses were canvassing near Bloomingdales. Then he invited both of the lovely ladies to be his guests for lunch. June didn't keep that date but he says he badgered her until she finally agreed to see him. He took her to church, then home to meet his family followed by dinner and a show. That man was determined! They became engaged the next month and married several months later. It was a joyous marriage and they and their family of four children remained in America and lived happy successful lives. June died in 2004, a victim of Alzheimer's disease.

Gloria remembers visiting her sister June in the fall of 1954, and being introduced to Herb shortly after the two had met. She thinks it was their third date, and Herb took them to a World Day of Prayer church service where Murray Ford, a Ney cousin's husband was preaching. She remembers it being a lovely drive and that Herb was a very charming man. When they finally got home that day the phone was ringing. Gloria's husband, Bob, had been frantically trying to reach her with some outstanding news. The Children's Aid Society had called to tell them that a 16-day-old wee boy was waiting for them to take home and cherish. What a thrilling message. Their prayers had been answered and Gloria hurried home as fast as she could to become the proud mother of Taylor John. Three years later on Dec. 28 1957 Margaret Louise (Marnie) joined them and their family was complete.

Marjorie, the third Bala Belfry daughter, married in Hamilton around that time too, and she and her husband, Art Madden, lived in Chatham. What a busy life they had. They were the proud parents of twin boys and twin girls as well as three other daughters; visitors were always welcome at their home too. What a busy household. Once when they arrived home after a busy day they were in the house about to eat dinner when the littlest one could not to be found. A diligent search began, only to find the babe still soundly sawing it off, but not in the bedroom, she was still buckled safely into the car seat outside in the car. I imagine they counted noses more often after that.

Uncle Arnim and Aunt Emily continued to be active over the years. Aunt Emily was a past master at making really superb maple syrup, and great wild strawberry and blueberry preserves. In the 1950s they moved into nearby Bala and this opened up a whole world of town living; church work, Ladies Aid, Women's Institute, and Lion's Club dinners.

Arnim and Emily Belfry, Bala

Visitors were welcome anytime, and I often enjoyed their hospitality the summer I worked at Bala. Uncle Arnim loved his workshop that he built after his garage was finished. Both of them revelled in living in God's country, Muskoka, regardless of which season of the year. It was all beautiful.

Doris and Leona (Lee), daughters of Mel and Olive, were growing up in Markdale where Doris trained to be a hairdresser and Lee was in high school Markdale is a pleasant town in Southern Ontario and they enjoyed life there. Often their weekends took them to the Victoria Harbour area, as Aunt Olive's Miller family came from that part of the country as well.

One of the happy activities of the summer of 1947 was an afternoon picnic gathering of the Belfry/Ney clan at Orillia, Ontario. As usual, the laughter and the camaraderie were front and centre.

The Belfry Family, Orillia, 1947
Back row: Arnim, Orin, Mel, Mert; Front row: Norm, Laura, Mother Belfry, Father Belfry, Roy

In March 1948 Mel was moved to Toronto as supervisor for the hydro lines in the Georgian Bay Area, and carried out his duties in Toronto until the new Regional Office at Barrie was ready for occupancy. Then he was promoted to Assistant Line Superintendent for the region and they busily prepared to sell their Markdale home and move to Barrie.

It was a hectic time as they gathered up their belongings and prepared to move that June. When they arrived in Barrie, Mel went into the downtown real estate office to sign the final documents for the purchase of their new home. His wife, our Aunt Olive, and daughter Lee had elected to wait in the car while he completed the formalities of the sale. As they sat there they saw some activity and an ambulance arrive on the scene. Of course they did not know what had happened, and because their move to Barrie was so recent no one knew them or how to contact them. Quickly Hydro personnel were contacted and one of their friends was able to search the street until he spotted them in the car. He then told them that Mel had suffered a coronary thrombosis and had died almost immediately. He was 53 years of age and had worked for the Hydro for 25 years.

What a dreadful shock for everyone. Waves of dismay and grief spread among their family and colleagues. I remember the disbelief on the face of our mother, Mary, as she received the call. Slowly she went to the garden to share the news with Norm that his beloved brother had died. Norm had been installed as Grand Master in the Masonic Lodge the night before and was catching his breath after the long evening and the lovely banquet Mary had provided. He was shocked as were the rest of the family and Hydro community. This first break among the brothers was a sad blow to all of them.

The gathering for Mel's funeral was a very sad one as Aunt Olive, Lee and Doris tried to absorb the fact that their life in this new community would be without Mel. Because the new Georgian Bay Regional Hydro offices were just opening and needed more personnel, Olive was asked if she would consider coming to work in the switchboard.

It sounded like a good way to become a part of her new environment as well as continue their Hydro association, so she readily accepted the offer. There she stayed for 19 years enjoying the camaraderie of many of their friends and seeing her brothers-in-law who were there for frequently meetings. The opportunity to be involved in this regional office made her an integral part of the Hydro which had been such a part of their lives for many years.

This photo appeared in the Hydroscope Magazine a few years later when it was realized that the Belfry clan was making an impact.
From left: Roy (Cannington), Olive (Barrie), Arnim (Bala), Lee (Personnel, Head Office) and Norm (Uxbridge)

In the Belfry family the oldest brother, Roy, was a powerful influence on his siblings and their families, too. They looked up to him, and following his example, many became respected Hydro employees in the following years. The Belfry family's collective working years held the record for family service in the history of the Georgian Bay Regional Area of the Ontario Hydro for many years, and I expect it still does. Records in the *Georgian Bayer,* the Hydro's annual publication, tells of this family's contribution to the development of Ontario Hydro. The 'Belfry Boys' together accumulated 182 years of service as follows: Roy 35 years, Arnim 39 years, Mel 25 years, Norm 44 years, Mert 13, and Orin 26. Most of this service was in the Georgian Bay Region.

If this was not impressive enough, the immediate family added many additional years: Mel's wife Olive 19 years as switch board operator in Barrie, their daughter Leona (Lee) seven years served in Personnel, Arnim's son Don worked both in Canada and Iran for a total of 37 years, Norm's son Ron four years on the line and his wife, Lillian, worked for nine years in offices in Kitchener and Richmond Hill on early computers. Orin's wife, Marion, worked in the Uxbridge and Owen Sound offices for six years. Laura, older sister of the boys, also helped contribute to this impressive record with her sons Jerry working 36 years and Mark 27 years in the business too. Gloria's husband, Bob, served 32 years and now their grandsons are adding to this record working as linemen in Southern Ontario. What a record!

Norm and Mary were finally able to move back to their own home in Uxbridge after the enforced sojourn in the apartment over the Hydro Office. While in the apartment our home was being rented by the High School principal and his family, and as we were both in school there, it did not seem wise to hurry them out unnecessarily. Finally they were able to find another home so we were delighted to move back. Then a flurry of redecorating made it our home again.

Cottage country was beginning to open up in Haliburton and Muskoka around this time, and some Uxbridge friends had already built summer homes on the wonderful northern Ontario lakes. These properties were Crown land, not unlike the ones available to our forefathers. After purchasing the land for a reasonable amount, some shelter needed to be erected within a year or so.

Our principal, Mr. Bernhardt, had a lovely piece of land available right beside his cottage and wondered if Mary and Norm would be interested. The Willis family, who were also good friends, had a small island just a stone's throw across the lake from the property in question, too. Little urging was needed for Mary and Norm to take a look at this beautiful place on Lake Kushog, and they fell in love with it at once. It was purchased and soon plans for a log cottage were made. Local loggers agreed to bring the logs across the bay when the ice was deep enough that winter. Such excitement! Mary and Norm could hardly wait till spring came so the cottage could be started. Then weekends were spent clearing the property and watching the cottage grow. While Norm worked on some of the outside clearing, Mary would take a mixture of sulfuric acid and water and scrub the stripped and installed logs till they glowed like honey.

Once during a log scrubbing, Mary and Norm stopped work and sat on them, surveying their kingdom while enjoying lunch. The logs were just high enough that they could sit comfortably and watch the lake as they ate. Such peace! Later that afternoon Mary could hear Norm chuckling away to himself. Finally her curiosity got the better of her and she asked him what the joke was. Imagine her chagrin when he informed her that the backside of her slacks had disintegrated. Oops! Perhaps that sulfuric acid mixture was just a touch too strong.

Lake Kushog cottage, 1948

The year 1949 progressed as it should. Mary remembers that was the year that Newfoundland voted to be part of the Confederation of Canada, our 10th province.

Although the cottage was finished and lovely, my brother and I were growing up and had other plans for the summer. My argument was that I would be going away to school in a couple of years and thought I should try my wings to see how they worked. This I explained in a school essay which garnered an A, and was then presented to my parents. After a great deal of discussion, they finally agreed to my request, and I loved being a waitress at Foxwood Inn in Muskoka as a waitress with two of

my friends. Ron had a great summer too which he spent sailing the Great Lakes on the *S. S. Manitoba,* which took passengers from Port McNicoll to the Lakehead, Fort William and Port Arthur and back again. He was the 'Silver King' which meant that he kept all of the utensils sparkling and ready for use. It was a great way to see some of the world and have fun at the same time. He sometimes helped the stevedore keep the coal furnace fed, too, to augment his salary. It gave him good muscles and was a good experience. Both Ron and I had enjoyed summer and truth to tell, we know our parents did, too.

Norm and Ron had another important task that year. Hydro was about to come to our Grandfather Hillis' farm near Hanover and it was an exciting prospect. Dad and Ron dug the post holes required to connect the main line on the road to the house, as each farmer was responsible for the installations on his own property. My brother remembers digging two postholes along the long driveway, and another one near the barn. This was done the hard way, one shovel full after another. Back breaking work indeed, but what a thrill it was to finally have electricity in that wonderful old home. Grandfather Hillis was a proud man the day it was finally completed, but Ron and our Dad were pretty proud as well.

By this time Norm was supervising two offices, one in Uxbridge and the other in Port Perry, but the area was well on its way to being fully serviced. On one of the regular business meetings in the area offices in Barrie he was presented with an interesting challenge. Would he consider moving to a larger area, in fact, go to Walkerton, where there was still growth potential? He and Mary had some serious thinking to do. Their home and gardens were finally the way they wanted them, they had marvelous friends, and the cottage was a comfortable distance for weekend visits.

On the other hand, Mary's father and two sisters lived in Hanover and Mildmay, not far from Walkerton. That was a big drawing card, and the job did sound interesting. They decided to take the challenge. I was certainly not as excited by this idea. I was a 16-year-old grade 13 student, involved in many activities, and I hated to leave my friends. But the die was cast and we moved.

Mary had been deeply involved in church work and other social and community activities and Norm had gone through the chairs in the Masonic Lodge, and been on local and area School Board executives, but they were rather excited by the idea of starting afresh.

Few houses were available in Walkerton so we rented while getting our bearings, and watched the market for a piece of property on which to build. Soon a lovely piece of property on South St. became available, filled the requirements and became ours.

Then the search was on for blueprints for a modern ranch style bungalow and a capable builder. This took some doing. Could they incorporate all their favorite things in one home? They had been in so many dwellings over the years that they had firm ideas about what their home should be like. Mary especially wanted kitchen cupboards that were comfortable for her 4-foot 11-inch frame. Yes, Norm saw that it was

done. It was their13th home and since their wedding day on 13 November long ago this number had been very lucky for them. It seemed that this was a good omen.

Construction continued under Norm's watchful eye, and to my surprise, they were already installed in a spanking new home when I came home from Teacher's College for Christmas 1951.

Life in the Fifties

Jean Fursman, Bea Harrison, Mary Belfry and Florence Hudson Circa 1950

Needless to say, Mary and her sisters were delighted to be living near each other after all of those years apart. Mary's home was about ten miles from each of her sisters so they were able to get together frequently. It was a perfect chance to rekindle their affection, and catch up on each other's lives.

Mary and Norm soon settled in, made friends and became actively involved in the community. Norm took up curling, joined Rotary and had his Masonic membership transferred to Walkerton. He was a volunteer driver for Cancer and Crippled Children and also headed their drive for funds for years.

Mary joined the Cancer Society and for the next 25 years made dressings twice monthly. She joined the Hobby Group whose motto was "Each one Teach one" and she did. She took oil painting, aluminum etching, copper work, leather craft and weaving. Then in turn she taught several of them including leather craft for three years. Finally a course in Fall Fair Judging started a whole new career in 1954. It was to continue until the late 1990s.

Mary's diaries tell about how much fun she had learning and then teaching many of these courses. Soon relatives and friends became the recipients of her amazing productivity. The urge to teach never left her, but it seems that it was not to be in the classroom. Rather, she taught children in Mission Band at church for many years. Frequently she was asked to be guest speaker at local or area United Church Women's meetings. She took executive positions in Women's Auxiliary activities, and was involved in Red Cross and Hospital Gift Shop activities, too.

She never lost her love of trees and flowers. In fact her diaries are well seasoned with enthusiastic descriptions of her beloved garden from early spring until it was clothed in sparkly snow drifts. She spoke of the vibrant autumn colours, sunshine and the moonlight on the water, and all of God's creatures.

To her surprise she was asked to take office in both Presbyterial and Conference work for the United Church and with Norm's urging did so. In this way many new friendships developed and they loved their new life in Walkerton.

One of the very popular activities in the Hanover and Walkerton communities were their Fall Fairs every autumn. Walkerton's was called The Little Royal, with a nod to the large Royal Winter Fair in Toronto. Mary loved all of the crafts, the baking and the flower arrangements that she remembered as such a part of her upbringing, and she usually saw old friends of the family each time she visited one. It began to feel like they had come full circle and that this was where they needed to be.

And so they settled into their new lives. Soon they realized that their Haliburton cottage was too far away for weekend enjoyment and reluctantly it was sold. How sad they were to lose such a beauty spot. However, Norm had become familiar with this new area in his work and realized that there was another lovely spot very near that might fill the bill.

Lake Rosyln, a man-made clutch of lakes, was nestled quietly about six miles away just off the Hanover road. One of their new friends had a summer place there so Mary and Norm were invited to have a look. Only one peek was needed and they decided that it would be a perfect spot to own. Granted, it didn't have the pines and the rocks of the previous one, but it did have a quiet lake, proximity to their home and friends near at hand.

Once again they were doing what they loved, planning for some special times in a new nest. They also realized that my brother and I would likely not be active participants in this new venture as we were growing up and away from home.

To their delight son Ron became engaged to Lillian Reilly of Waterloo and this was a thrill for them as they contemplated having another daughter in our family.

Belfry Cottage, Lake Rosyln

Ron had been working in Waterloo and he kept seeing this lovely girl waiting for her bus at the stop across the street from where he waited. He was intrigued so asked around to find out who she was. After finally working up his nerve he introduced himself. It seems in this family that important heart-interests make themselves known with little delay, and soon they were an item. Lillian Reilly worked in the Hydro office in Waterloo. What? Could there be yet another Belfry added to this Hydro clan? It was beginning to sound like this disease was catching. Lillian visited often on the weekends and soon became a beautiful part to our family.

We were all delighted and their wedding in April 1956 was a joyous occasion. They continued to be regular weekend visitors to house and cottage over the years and having them there were bright moments for Norm and Mary.

Ron and Lillian Reilly Belfry, 1956

Changes were taking place with the older generation, too. Our Grandfather Belfry had a heart attack and died as a result in May of 1951. It was a prolonged illness and his children were relived that he no longer would suffer. We remember him sitting at his favorite chair by the window overlooking Georgian Bay, smoke curling from the pipe he clutched in his mouth and his frequent use of 'Merci' and other French phrases.

In Mary and Norm's home Grandmother Belfry became a winter visitor. We do remember that this habit had already been started by an earlier Belfry who visited around with his children, and this became our grandmother's habit as well. Grandmother Belfry came to call on a rotational basis, not unlike our forefather Jacob Belfry. She enjoyed the companionship and spent the rest of her life this way. And we enjoyed her company when we were home for a visit. Senior residences were not yet in vogue so families were the ones who shouldered the responsibility.

Several years later our Grandfather Hillis in Hanover suffered a stroke and became bedridden so he too needed care. He was ill for a many months and the sisters took turns assisting his wife Jessie. He died at Christmas time 1955 with his daughters around him. We are reminded that the social services on which we have come to depend were still not available. Families became the caregivers if possible and often the nighttime care became very hard on everyone.

With the exception of three years in Brampton, our Grandfather Hillis had lived all of his life in the same family home. What an interesting man he was. His humour showed in the constant twinkle in his eyes, and the goofy letters he wrote that started from the outside of the paper, continued around the page in a circle, and then reconstructed the spiral back from the inside out. When finally deciphered, you knew that you had had a message from a loved man who was chuckling all the while he was writing it.

After our grandfather's death Mary's older sister, Florence, and husband, Emerson, bought the high ceiling, eleven-room Hillis homestead that James Hillis had built in 1882. What joy it was for her to come back home again. Her life, too, seemed to have come full circle.

Sister Florence was the consummate farm wife and helpmate. She had joined the Hanover Agricultural Society in 1926 soon after her marriage to Emerson Hudson, and he joined the following year. Both of their families had shown horses in Hanover's very first Hanover Fair, and this participation continued for four generations, with their son Jack following in their footsteps. Florence also exhibited flowers, baking and canning for many years, always capturing many colourful ribbons as prizes.

The Hillis and Hudson families had lived on neighbouring farms and on Florence and Emerson's marriage they bought one of the Hudson properties and this is where they lived for first 34 years of their married lives.

Their family of three boys, Jack, Jim and Gary, and their families have lived in nearby farms all of their lives as have many of their grandchildren. They happily celebrated their 60th Anniversary in 1982. They had lived all of their lives on family homesteads in the area and were highly respected members of the community.

Emerson, Florence, Jim, Jack and Gary Hudson, '77

As well as their three sons they were grandparents of eight and great grandparents of six children. Both were avid gardeners and especially loved flowers. Their participation in Agricultural Societies in Brant, Bentinck and Hanover and the Hanover Horticultural Society was noteworthy as well. Florence also took up nursing duties in Durham for a number of years, which she thoroughly enjoyed. Her energy seemed to know no bounds.

The Hillis sisters Jean, Mary, Florence and Bea celebrate Florence's Golden Anniversary

Sadly, Aunt Florence, following years of work on the farm, as a nurse at Durham Hospital and as an active member of the community, was forced to spend her last years in Hanover Hospital as a victim of Alzheimer's. During one hospital visit long after she had forgotten how to speak, I reminded her of what a special meal that pork tenderloin dinner that she had served us years before had been for us. All at once her body started to rock and a wonderful smile broke over her face. We are quite sure that she remembered the farm and the joy she took in being there. It was a special, touching moment for all of us.

Mary's sister Beatrice lived in Mildmay, just a few miles to the south of Walkerton. There she and her husband, Oliver Harrison, raised four children, three boys: Earl, Ross and Alan, and a daughter: Jeanne Marie, later known as Jean. Most of her children remained in Southern Ontario, with short adventures off to Elliot Lake or other areas in the north.

Aunt Beatrice was an amazing woman who approached each challenges with a smile. Her formula for cheerfulness was, "If you keep saying it's not going to get you down, it won't." She used this motto when she survived two heart attacks, leukemia, cancer of the spleen and a paralytic stroke, and carried her through the untimely deaths of a son and four grandsons.

She was heard to say that she had done the work of a farmer, a seamstress, a store clerk, bookkeeper, antique dealer and even a preacher once when a quick fill-in was necessary. She proudly displayed her kitchen cupboard, ones she had installed herself complete with the electrical wiring. She, like Mary, was a recorder and apparently had kept a written record of everything she had spent on her family from her marriage in 1928. What a woman!

She and Uncle Oliver celebrated their Golden Anniversary in June of 1978 in Mildmay, where they had lived their whole married life. Unfortunately his health deteriorated and he died the next year.

Aunt Bea was a whirlwind at whatever she did and was an important part of the town of Mildmay. We remember her joie de vivre, and visiting her was always a fun thing to do. She and Mary both took an active part in their church activities and more than once spoke in each other's women's association activities.

Celebrating their 50th Anniversary with children Alan, Jean and Ross

Mary's third sister, Jean, was still living in Toronto with her husband, Charles Fursman, when they decided it was time to sell their very large home on Ellerbeck and move to an apartment. They chose one on Woodbine and were on the move when Charles slipped on the sidewalk and hit his head on the cement. He was rushed to the hospital, where he underwent medical treatment for some time.

Jean and Charles Fursman

It was a difficult time for Jean but Mary came to help her, and together they were able to set up the new apartment and help Charles become comfortable when he was able to be moved. Slowly he became more active again but was never quite as agile as he had been before his accident.

In the interim years, Norm's brother Mert and his wife, Marg, had become the proud owners of Meadow Springs Lodge near Bobcagon. They enjoyed their new life style and it was a wonderful place to bring up their two children, Maribeth and Larry.

Mert and Marg, and Maribeth and Larry at Meadow Springs

It was also a great place for a family party and that was where we all gathered to celebrate Mary and Norm's 25th wedding anniversary. It was a lovely party with all of the Belfry clan sharing in the festivities.

Ron and Lillian were excited about purchasing a new home in Waterloo and had just moved into it when Ron's company moved him to Toronto. Then a couple of quick business moves happened. They found themselves selling what they thought would be their dream home, buying one in the suburb of Mississauga, and then cancelling this one for another home in Richmond Hill because of Lillian's transfer there. Her expertise in using the Hydro's computer system was a big asset and that was where she was needed. Whew! What a flurry.

Mary and Norm's 25th Anniversary

This all took a matter of months to settle so Ron took over the basement family room in the home that I shared with Althea Collins, a fellow teacher in East York. We were glad to have a 'roomie' who could fix leaky taps and see to any plumbing problems, and he was delighted to have a place to hang his hat during the week.

In 1957 Mary's diary tells us that the Russians launched a second satellite, this time with a dog in it. She also tells of my first trip to Europe and my exciting nine weeks of travel in a Morris Minor with three girlfriends. They were fascinated with all the preparations, and Mom and I were really giddy on the drive to Malton for my first ever flight. I remember very sweaty hands and not wanting to touch any of my new clothes. As only a mother would do, she suggested that I dry my hands on her slip. And I did! Norm was quietly driving as we clacked and giggled so I asked him if he wasn't just a little bit excited. To this he replied quietly that indeed there was one small butterfly attempting to fly in his tummy.

Later as our flight was taking off, Mary turned to say something to him, and there on his shoulder, was one small butterfly preparing to launch. It seemed prophetic somehow.

Interesting enough, cousin Lee, Mel and Olive's daughter was also about to go off on an adventure to another land. Surely there must be wanderlust in the bones of my Belfry cousins because many of us either took off for parts unknown, or have travelled quite extensively to other climes.

Lee Belfry Bryen and Ken Bryen in 2001

In Lee's case, she had been working for the Hydro in personnel in various places, with extended trips to interesting spots every so often. While on a trip out west she was offered a posting in White Dove Falls, north of Kenora, Ontario. It sounded like a good place to salt a few pennies away for further travels so she decided to take it just for the adventure. As luck would have it, while there she met a handsome young man from Australia who was working as a surveyor in the area. Did Ken Bryen really fall off that cliff accidentally so he would end up in the hospital near where Lee was working, allowing them to meet or did the fates trip him? Whatever happened, meet they did and before too long they decided to marry and head for Australia.

In the late 1950s one didn't hop on a plane, spend 24 hours in the air, and then arrive slightly baggy eyed in the Land Down Under. Ken and Lee took an ocean liner. Lee says they made a number of stops along the American west coast, San Francisco being one of them, then they stopped at Hawaii, then in Fiji and Auckland, Sydney and finally Melbourne, which was near where they were headed. One of their Hydro friends later was heard to say that they really did have their honeymoon on a "slow boat to China".

They lived and worked there for several years and now live in Lakefield, Ontario. Their family of three boys: Scott, Neal and Chris, and one daughter:Shelly, has grown and they have six grandchildren, three boys and three girls.

Lee's sister Doris had married Bob Burke and they lived with their six children in Barrie. This is where they retired and now enjoy having their children and seven grandchildren living nearby.

As the 1950s were rolling to a close, Mary and Norm were facing a wonderful new experience, the chance to be grandparents.

Ron and Lillian were thrilled that they were to become parents. Knitting needles clicked as they eagerly awaited her arrival. Amid great excitement Colleen Margaret arrived on 30 November and everyone was simply delighted. From then on she held the heartstrings of all of her grandparents. And aunts and uncles, too! A perfect way to head into the next decade and Mary and Norm were ready to throw themselves into the task of being perfect grandparents.

The Sixties

The sixties were sneaking up on the world awash in psychedelic colours, jazzy music and freedom from some of the confines of the more Victorian past. Life was rolling along at a delightful clip but our Grandmother Belfry had one small concern. Two of her grown grandchildren were still not married! This was not the way it used to be and she began to think that she should be worried about cousin Don and me.

Don Belfry, Arnim and Emily's only son who was another Hydro recruit was working in Sudbury as an operator and marriage had so far eluded him. However, some mutual friends of Don's and a charming Physical Health teacher named Bobbie Beeton, who taught in Sudbury High School decided that these two should meet at an early summer dinner party. Meet they did and both Don and Bobbie were charmed. Soon Don was introduced to widowed Bobbie's two children, eight-year-old Lynn and six-year-old Glenn, and found them a lovely extension of their mother. Then Bobbie met Don's parents and sisters. Everyone was sure that this was a match made in heaven, especially the two major players. To great cheers of excitement Don and Bobbie announced that would marry in August, 1960. What a touching wedding it was. In offering a toast at the reception, Don spoke of his pride in becoming a loving husband *and* a happy father all in one fell swoop. It was a delightful moment.

That wasn't the only fascinating chapter in their lives. In 1962 Don and a team of ten Canadians were invited to go to Iran to train operators in using electrical equipment in Italian-built dams in the southwest. The new family were thrilled to see that part of the world and loved the experience. Some adjustments were needed to live in the sometimes 130 degree temperature. House hold help was provided and there was a large communal pool for those in the compound. Here Bobbie shone. Her Phys Ed training gave her the skills to teach First Aid and she also taught swimming to those interested.

Many were, and they all had a wonderful time putting on swim shows, and even ventured a version of South Pacific.

What a different way of life it was. No TV, lots of reading and only one English newspaper a week. They were asked not to add to their family while there, as medical facilities were unavailable, but nature has a way of changing plans. Their daughter, Jane Ellen, was born there in 1961and a son, Brian Earl, joined the ranks in 1963. The family had a second tour there from 1970 to 1972 when Don was the Superintendent in a team of two. It was a great way to see exotic parts of the world. We imagine they must hear present day political happenings with much concern about how both the people and the landscape have been affected.

And that left me with my itchy feet and love of travel. My marvelous first trip to Europe had opened up a whole new world for me and whetted my appetite for more. After some soul searching I decided to apply for a teaching position with the Department of National Defense. Soon I asked East York for permission to go on loan for a two year posting to Europe and it was granted in 1959. Teachers were chosen from all the provinces and I was fortunate enough to be one of them. What excitement! Although I had applied to go to Germany, I learned that I would be in Marville, France and soon trunks were being readied for my new adventure. My parents, Mary and Norm were excited, too, but quite likely they had some quiet reservations about what the two years would bring.

I imagine my ocean crossing in First Class opulence on the *S.S. Italia* was vastly different from those experienced by my forefathers some generations before. They also didn't have the comfort of a new car awaiting them on arrival as I did.

My brand-new two-toned black and white Simca awaited me in Paris, and my new life in France was about to unfold. How thrilling. However, I did make one important decision as I sat at the wheel that first morning. In hopes that my shiny fenders would be intact when I reached the other side of the City of Light, I carefully studied the map. Next I slowly drove to the right bank of the Seine, and slowly, very slowly hugged the river bank as it wound through the edge of the city to exit on the eastern side. No terrifying broad open boulevards in central Paris for me that morning. My car was still unscathed as I set off to meet my destiny.

My adventure turned into a chance to make many new friends, led me on Day One to meet a certain Bill Lynn, the handsome Sabre pilot from Montreal destined to become my loving husband, and offered amazing opportunities to explore so many fascinating corners of the world.

Mom's letters to me were full of precious Colleen, the details of each new stage of development, and her first smiles and words. Mine told of all of the interesting sights of this fascinating country, of weekend jaunts to London, Munich, Paris and Switzerland and even a holiday in Egypt and the Holy Land. I also described the wonderful foods and festivals, and the person that had stolen my heart.

Norm and Mary had been hearing all about Bill but could not be encouraged to come to Europe to meet him until we invited them to our wedding to be celebrated in late 1960. That did convince them and they made their plans. It was to be Mary's first flight and naturally she was very anxious.

What excitement when I picked them up at the airport in Luxembourg the week before our wedding. It was all so different and thrilling for both of them. The city of Luxembourg was festive, but first and foremost they were anxious to meet their new son-in-law. And meet him they did, and very much liked what they saw. The week followed with several bridal showers, dinners, parties, getting acquainted time and much laughter as we prepared for our special day.

An interesting aspect of French law required that a civil wedding take place before a church ceremony, and ours was held in the Mayor's office in Marville, the small 8th century town near the Base. Our parents, colleagues and many friends joined us there as we became man and wife. To us it was a unique part of our meeting and living in France.

Revisiting the Mayor's Office, Marville, France 2005

Dennis and Marg Paproski, our wedding attendants, the present mayor, and Marg and Bill Lynn back where we had celebrated our civil ceremony

The mayor, festooned with regal ribbons of office, rattled off a long litany of French, including our parents' names, domiciles, and much more. All very official, and all impressive! Following that, a sumptuous banquet called a Dining-In Night for all officers and their families was enjoyed at the #1 Wing Air Force Station. Mary and Norm were so pleased to be a special part of that elegant affair.

The next day our religious ceremony was celebrated at the Protestant Chapel with many friends and my family to cheer us on. Chaplain Wilson Yates, the base chaplain officiated. Norm and Mary were staying at a little inn in nearby Longuyon and the bathtub nearly undid Norm the morning of the wedding. It was perched high on four legs and Norm nearly broke his toe while getting in. However, he just grinned and walked tall as he escorted me down the aisle to become Bill's bride.

A four-sabre fly-past was arranged by some of Bill's 441 squadron friends and was to soar over the chapel as we made our exit as newlyweds, but overhead the clouds hung low and it was considered too dangerous to attempt. Then off we went to our reception in a checkerboard bedecked car escorted by Bill's buddies wearing black bowlers and black roses on their lapels.

Protestant chapel, #1 Air Division Base, France Norm Belfry, Dennis Paproski, Bill and Marg Lynn, Marg Paproski and Mary Belfry

Our reception was held in the wood paneled 'Stag Room' of the Officer's Mess, after which we left for Austria and Switzerland.

While in Europe my parents toured Brussels, Paris and London and were awed by the whole experience, especially the week in our small corner of France. The major cities were wonderful and they explored them on foot and on tours.

But for them the real essence of the trip was living in a little village, going to the daily markets, seeing how people in another country carry out their day to day existence, and helping us get married.

Mary particularly liked to tell about ordering sandwiches for lunch at the inn in Longuyon, likely picturing a ham and cheese on brown, and receiving the typical mile long baguette stuffed with local ham, cheese and crudities. "It could have fed an army!" she was heard to say. She told about a visit to Croix Rouge, a Belgian inn where whole families gathered to visit. Imagine children, parent, and grandparents all sharing an afternoon of music, wine and laughter in an inn on a Sunday afternoon! Europeans really did have interesting customs, but some European washrooms were a bit of a surprise.

Year-old Colleen was waiting at the airport with her parents on their return. When Colleen spied them her excitement reached fever pitch and her verbal enthusiasm delighted everyone. What a marvelous homecoming!

Now our Grandmother Belfry could relax. All of her grandchildren were married.

And in that next year Ron and Lillian's second daughter, Joanne Lillian, made her appearance as did our daughter, Heather-Anne Lynn, dual citizen of France and Canada, who brightened our home and garden in Virton, Belgium.

By late 1962 we learned that we were soon to be posted to Collège Militaire Royal in St Jean Quebec. Such excitement as we prepared for our return. Our reunion with new kids and family to meet was very special.

Our Grandmother Belfry, in her early 90s and in failing health, finally lost her battle at Owen Sound Hospital in the fall of 1963. She was laid to rest beside her beloved husband Sherman in the Victoria Harbour Cemetery, near a number of other Belfrys who were also at rest.

Our Grandparent's funeral monument, Victoria Harbour Cemetery

The next two years were busy ones as our parents visited back and forth and our families again increased in size. In our home we welcomed Brian Alexander in February, the first grandson for all four of his grandparents and in May, Ron and Lillian welcomed Wanda June, their third daughter.
Five grandchildren to love, and love them they did.

Retirement

Norm was reaching his 65th year and in September of 1964 he celebrated his retirement from the Hydro after 44 years in their service.

As one of the most senior of their team he was widely feted and his success over the years was honoured. Many of those working in offices and construction teams had been hired and trained under his watch and they wanted him to know how much his support and encouragement had meant to them. These men were friends and remained so for the rest of his life.

Many accolades and gifts were received and he was especially delighted with the power tools which allowed him to custom make his own cedar paneling to line the extension on their cottage. And what did he use to make the paneling? He had purchased unused hydro poles and those strong, tall poles provided the cedar. How fitting!

With an enlarged family he though more space would be an advantage. He was right, and this became a great way for Norm to ease out of the day-to-day business of an office manager and become his own boss. And the lovingly improved cottage became a haven for their children and grandchildren in the years to come.

Likely there were times when he relived his Hydro years, but one of his most delightful memories was of the day he donned business suit and brief case, climbed into his bright red canoe beside the cottage and went off to oversee his construction team who were installing power lines across the lake.

Mary and Norm loved to travel the highways and byways of the land, especially the quiet roads beside small rivers and lakes. With this in mind they bought a small house trailer. With the canoe atop their car off they went to explore the great west in early fall of 1965 for their retirement trip.

However, before they did that they came to help us move from St. Jean to Lachine so that Bill could begin his career as an Electrical Engineer. It was seven years since his graduation from RMC and McGill and he was anxious to do what he had originally trained for. Their expertise in moving was amazing. Down came the curtains, the hardware and various extras, away they went with a carload *and* our two children, and the next thing we knew all were installed in our new home when we arrived with the moving van. Whew! Experience really *is* a good teacher.

Then they hit the open road to experience the rest of Canada. The three month experience allowed them to visit many cousins in the west. Uncle Harvey Switzer, Mary's grandfather's brother, was a pharmacist in Edson Alberta and he and his fourteen children dotted the landscape across the west. What fun they had finally getting to know cousins with whom they had been corresponding for years. These cousins so enjoyed meeting that many of them kept in touch by visit and letters over the ensuing years. Our parents also refreshed themselves beside lovely quiet lakes, were awed by the grandeur of the Rockies and the vastness of the Yukon, and truly tasted the beautiful Canadian landscape. It was an amazing experience for both of them.

At home the busy schedule of their lives was taken up again but they relived the trip often as they looked at their slides and remembered the time spent with absent family members.

Norman A Belfry

Mary M Belfry

They had loved the trailer but found it superfluous on returning home so gave it to us on their next visit. From then on the Eastern Seaboard, the mountains and lakes in widening circles were at our beck and call. What fun we had. We four used it happily until a shoehorn was needed to accommodate us and our growing children.

Mary's diaries tell us that 1968 was a busy year on the world stage. She says, "This 1968 has been a year of violence and destruction. Martin Luther and Senator Robert Kennedy were assassinated, there were race riots in Chicago, students revolted and hippies ruled. It was also the year of the first heart transplant, the year man walked on the moon and the year Nancy Green captured the gold medal in the Olympics. As well it was the year of the mini skirt and the year Russia invaded Czechoslovakia". Yes indeed, a year to remember!

As the decade rolled on to a close she speaks of more violence, robberies and drug abuse. Her annual compilation of world events in the last pages of her diaries is an interesting capsule of historic events, and reminds us that she was an astute, caring member of society.

Mary and Norm took much pleasure in the accomplishments of their growing family, loved visiting and reading bedtime tales, telling the children stories of their childhood, and were there to applaud dance recitals, musical activities and graduations.

It seemed that life was mellow for our family until one fateful Sunday in early July of 1974. A new cedar hydro pole had just been lowered into position at the cottage to supply the increasing needs for their cottage and others nearby. Brother Ron was now the owner and manager of this family's summer home, giving Norm one less home to oversee.

Norm looked longingly at the pole, remembered his beginning as a lineman, and decided he'd like the thrill of climbing a pole once more. All the necessary spurs and safety equipment were nearby and so, using all necessary precautions, he did just that. What a thrill for him to view the lake from above and wave at his cheering family.

Later that afternoon he was being troubled by some chest pain and Ron suggested that they take a short spin into Walkerton to the Hospital to check things out. Reluctantly Norm agreed, with the proviso that they stop at the house first so he could put on something a little less casual than his shorts.

This was done. The diagnosis was an aneurism in his aorta and he was rushed by ambulance to the Victoria Hospital, London, Ontario. Long surgery ensued with numerous transfusions and intensive care, but he had suffered massive damage and died the next evening in his 75th year.

Mary was devastated, as were we all.

We wondered just how she would be able to pick up the threads of her life without the warm support of her love, but her resilience shone through and she did. Not only did she manage, but she managed to stay in her own home for the next 26 years. Happy visits were made to Quebec, Hawaii, California and other locals with friends and relatives. She even took a cruise with Mabe Parslow Eade, her dear friend from Normal School days. Friends and neighbours were always a very special part of her life and they nourished each other in those years when they were on their own again.

Summers offered the time for extended visits and Mary and I often visited Stratford for Shakespeare or Blythe for B&Bs and little theatre. These were bright spots in Mary's life and in mine, too. We explored old haunts, fond holiday locations and paid visits to the remaining sisters-in law. On a visit to see Aunt Emily in Midland we found that she had just been placed in the hospital for observation. Emily's delightful sense of humour shone through when she suggested to her daughter Marjorie that they tell Mary that she had just dropped in for the day. Those two spunky Belfry gals had a good laugh at the hoped for subterfuge. What a marvelous pair of women they were.

All of the sisters-in-law were on their own by now and being with them and hearing the affection in their voices as they remembered was very special. What a treat it was to sit back and listen to them become young again.

The Eighties and Nineties

Mary surprised everyone by her ability to maintain her home, keep her beloved garden looking beautiful and continue preserving her favorite jams, conserves and relishes. Friends and relatives often dropped in for tea, or for a game of bridge and her well stocked freezer always produced succulent delicacies. When she needed a lift she would bake several pans of goodies and then pack them into her freezer with a tasty selection in each package. Later, when someone came to call her choice was taken out and nicely thawed by the time they were ready for tea.

Gradually she let down barriers and asked for help but most of the time her independence was front and centre. She loved working in the Gift Shop at the hospital and taking part in all the social activities around. She helped make Christmas baskets for shut-ins well into her 80s, not realizing that she, too, was in that category. Kind neighbours brought the mail to her door and took her to church each Sunday. Her diaries speak of the joy of each day, and how much her family and her memories meant to her. And how much she loved the beautiful changing seasons!

By now her grandchildren were leaving home for further studies, but they always kept in touch and visited when they could. She was used to all her granddaughters as Ron's girls were able to pop in regularly when visiting their parents, who had moved to Hanover on retirement, or were at the cottage. Our daughter, Heather, now studying in Toronto, was closer at hand, too. How she loved their visits. But she was rather surprised when Brian, her 17-year-old only grandson from Montreal, called to see if he could come for a weekend before beginning his university studies at Harvard. How would she manage to entertain and feed a 17-year-old boy? It turned out to be no problem at all and they were both thrilled with the fun and affection they shared.

This special affection shone through in 1988 when Brian and the love of his life, Janet Fryer, became engaged at elegant 'The Belfry Restaurant' in Stratford Ont. Was it a tip of the hat to Brian's forefathers that inspired him to choose that location to ask Janet to marry him? They went to Walkerton to visit Grandma Belfry the next day and she was the first to be told of their plans. As requested she kept the delightful news to herself until we four parents were finally let in on the secret. We were all thrilled that Janet would be part of our lives, and Mary's eyes flashed as they gave each other a 'thumbs up' in the receiving line at their wedding.

By 1986 the granddaughters were married and Heather and John's daughter ,Raya Lynn, was adding to Grandma Great's bouquet of loved ones. Our children called her Little Grandma Great to differentiate between their two Grandmothers, and Grandma Great Lynn also enjoyed the charming name.

Wanda, Colleen, Joanne

Janet and Brian

Heather and John

At that time Mary was encouraged to write down some of the stories of her childhood so that Raya and the great-grandchildren to come would be able to appreciate how life had been when she was a child. It turned out to be a labour of love and Mary had such fun writing about all the different aspects of her growing up years that had shaped her life.

Mary's memoirs were printed and given to her family in February 1991 when we were gathered together to celebrate our daughter, Heather's, 'Call to the Bar'. Mary was thrilled and excited to see her words in print as were all the recipients.

Her closing words at that time were very touching:

The little path I started in 1907 has now become a well trodden road. I learned that the greatest thing in the world is LOVE. Love for your God, your spouse, your children, your neighbours and the world at large.

We had a wonderful marriage for forty-six years, then very suddenly, I was left alone. And once more life changed!

I still live in my own home, do my own work, and am surrounded by love.

I have lived through no phone, no radio, television, toilet paper, Kleenex, pasteurized milk or plastic containers. I have lived through the Depression, two world wars, watched man's first step on the moon, and the possibility of nuclear war. And in spite of all this, some things haven't changed. The sun still sets every evening, the morning dew still glistens on the grass, the robin still sings in the rain, the golden wheat fields still ripple with the wind, and four glorious seasons are still with us.

Through living I have learned courage, faith, strength, compassion and love, and LOVE is the greatest thing in life.

This is my story. I hope it gives you an insight into my life, and perhaps you could even learn a little from it.

My love to all my great grandchildren

Your Great Grandmother Belfry.

There were still many things for Mary to accomplish so she continued her involvement with church, neighbours, friends, and family. Sister Jean was the only one of her sisters or brothers-in law still living, as many other loved ones had died. Mary felt their loss very much.

Ron, a Senior Consultant with the Construction Safety Association of Ontario, decided on early retirement and he and Lillian planned a move to Hanover. What was more, they convinced Aunt Jean, Mary's special sister, to move to Hanover as well. What a marvelous lift for Mary's spirits and for Aunt Jean's as well. For the next few years the two sisters were able to chat daily on the phone, visit often and cherish each time they could be together.

Mary Belfry and Jean Fursman

Those next years were very busy ones for Ron and Lil as they shopped, ran errands and assisted Mary and Jean with many, many tasks. Lil was a marvelous cook and often arrived with tasty individual meals for their freezers. What a wonderful gift of time this represented and was so much appreciated, especially by the sisters when dinnertime rolled around.

Ron would take Mary and Jean to appointments on time, pick up groceries or medication, take them to the market, or just visit. The sisters felt so cherished.

My summer trips with Mary now included Aunt Jean and my dear friend Rosalie Macfarlane who had 'adopted' Aunt Jean when she lived in Toronto. Our foursome visited Cullen Gardens and loved the glorious flowers of which Mary was so fond. Stratford, with all of the delights of the theatres and boutiques was a special yearly happening while possible. These two wonderful women never hesitated at a given suggestion. Could we fit in a fashion show with lunch before a matinee? No question at all. Each outing became a marvelous adventure for all of us, and Rosalie and I felt blessed to be able to share such beautiful experiences.

Aunt Jean was very frail and had been suffering from leukemia for a number of years. Finally in the summer of 1995 when she was severely weakened by the disease, she entered the hospital in Hanover. Again Mary was to sit with a loved one and be helpless to change the course of history. However, she could remind her beloved sister of their happy childhood on the farm and the joy their marriages had brought them. Those days were special times for our cousins and our family to sit with Aunt Jean when we recalled happy occasions and shared our affection. She died in early September 1995.

Jean's passing left a decided void in Mary's life but she stoically remained involved in the world around her. She was helped considerably by a caring home helper, Janice Lippert who came several hours every few day to supervise her bath, tidy the house and prepare things for Mary's comfort. Janice was a breath of fresh air and helped keep an eye on Mary's welfare. She was a constant warm friend and was much appreciated by all of us as she helped Mary remain as self sufficient as she did.

Reading was a constant joy for Mary and she continued to enjoy local and international news, good literature and poetry. She watched her family grow, following each one through their school days and took great delight in each accomplishment.

Mary's 90th birthday party in February 1997 was a time for friends and relatives to shower her with affection, and she loved the many cards, flowers and memories that each one brought. She was a happy, fulfilled woman who cherished life.

Mary with children Marg and Ron

Her family kept in close touch with daily phone calls. She wore a monitor but we did worry about the frequent times when we couldn't reach her. Small strokes continued but she was adamant that she was well able to stay in her home.

About the third week of May 2000, Walkerton was lambasted by terrible rainstorm. Most of the nearby countryside was inundated. She described the storm in our nightly phone conversation as one of the worst she had ever seen. I was planning to visit her a few days later and she admonished me to watch the weather and be careful on the roads, her constant reminder before I travelled.

As I neared the town I was awestruck by the vast pools of water lying everywhere. Cows were standing captive surrounded by brand new lakes, rivers, ponds and culverts were overflowing, and the countryside was totally saturated. Yes, there had indeed been a monstrous storm.

We were well into a marvellous visit catching up on the world and ourselves a few days later when my cousin Jean Liesemer called to see how her Aunt Mary was. And even how I was! Of course we said we were both fine, except I had noted to myself that I was experiencing a little traveller's complaint. Because I had been in transit for a few days prior to arriving in Walkerton, I wasn't concerned. Then Jean told us that quite a number of local folks were heading to the hospital with a nasty bug of some kind. This was our first inkling that a major problem was rearing its head.

The next day as we left the local Tim Horton's after church, the restaurant closed its doors to customers, and was to stay closed for quite some time. "Very strange!" we thought as we headed home. Many other establishments in town were to follow suit in the coming days too. This badly affected the economy in Walkerton which was to suffer from this turn of events. As many of us know now, a very serious strain of E-coli had seeped into the water system and this resulted in a number of illnesses and deaths. Then and later many townsfolk and visitors were affected in a number of life altering ways, and the town reeled with the enormity of the situation. My own discomfort continued off and on for the next weeks but was in no way comparable to the many lives which were permanently changed in the weeks and months to come.

It was not an easy time for anyone who lived there. Those huge bottles of water delivered daily to their doors were too heavy for many of the older residents to pick up, the roar of the helicopter delivering patients to the hospital was traumatic, and each time they heard the ambulance scream by they wondered which of their friends had fallen ill. Stress, a constant companion, was taking a heavy toll on everyone.

Mary was no exception. She was hospitalized in early August with some of the same symptoms suffered by those affected, but as she was in her 93rd year, they could possibly have been the ramifications of her age and the stressful atmosphere pervading in the town. Because she had become so frail, Dr. Creighton, her friend and physician for decades, felt it was finally necessary for her to move to a senior's residence where she could have regular care and support.

Mary was not happy about this situation, feeling that she was still completely able to manage on her own. It is interesting that our analytical skills sometimes play tricks on us. Mary didn't realize that the small strokes along the way had caused some permanent damage and thus diminished her reasoning powers. She did move to a residence, much against her better judgement but was devastated to have to leave her beloved home.

Short weeks later she was again hospitalized, and there she died within our arms on 25 September 2000.

She was the last living daughter and daughter-in-law of the Belfry and Hillis clans, and had certainly earned her rest.

Her own journey through life expressed as written to her great-grandchildren in 1985, was shared by the minister during her funeral service. She was a happy, fulfilled woman who had been greatly loved.

Now she and our father Norman Belfry share shade under a spreading maple tree in Walkerton Cemetery. It is a quiet, peaceful place that Mary herself chose.

Walkerton Cemetery

What a rich partnership and loving circle they forged.

Her spunk and good humour shines as she shares her uplifting approach to life with those who will become the children of tomorrow.

Mary's Postscript

These words were written in 1999, mere months before the Walkerton crisis, which hastened her death.

Dear Great-Grandchildren,

*I see that it is 14 years since I wrote a little book to you folks about my life – and thought **that** would be it. But, in June of this year my old high school in Hanover had its first reunion since inception in 1924. 200 students were registered. It was a three-day celebration and I was able to attend two sessions, which I will never forget. I thought you might like to hear about it.*

*When the high school opened in 1924 the motto was **'Enter to Learn–Go Forth to Serve'**. I didn't realize what an impact that had on so many lives (mine included). That church service I shall never forget. The school band provided the music. The choir, close to 100 voices, had all been Hanover High School pupils. The worship leader was a ministry student of the Presbyterian Church of Canada.*

Photo taken for *The Hanover Post,* **1999**

Speakers were a Professor of Pastoral Care and Counseling of Waterloo Lutheran Seminary and two retired United Church ministers, all of whom had gradu ated from Hanover High School.

Even the ushers and those who took up the offering were former graduates. Such a variety of talent! These had all gone out to serve from the school. There had been nine principals from 1924 to 1999 and all were there but two who were deceased. I came home from that service thinking I was well blessed to have had a year of my life there, and to have been able to learn and go forth to serve.

I have told you some of my life in my first memoir so perhaps I should fill you in as to my life since then.

In 1982 I had a heart attack, which put me in hospital for six weeks and slowed me up a bit, but I was still able to continue my church and hospital work. This year I received my Life Membership in hospital work, both in the Auxiliary and on the Gift Shop Executive, and my 35-year pin for UCW (United Church Women).

Life went on…volunteer work, bridge, teas, friends dropping in, playing the solitary bridge game in the paper every day, enjoying my garden, and you, my great grandchildren.

Now I'll give you a bit of 'old age know-it-all'. If you are ever told to go to a doctor–don't put it off. I didn't go, and one morning I woke up to find everything in my living room and out doors a soft shade of green. I blinked my eyes but it didn't change for about 15 minutes. I decided I should see my eye doctor because I have had cataracts removed twice, and found that I had glaucoma in my one eye. So, off to the Doctor I went. He said there was nothing the matter with my eye but I should see my medical doctor about a vein in my neck.

Well, that was the middle of December and the busiest time of the year with bazaars, teas, special Christmas activities and I didn't have time for a doctor.

After Christmas I took a stroke and that DID slow me down for another six weeks in bed. After that, WOW, exercises for a half an hour every morning trying to move my feet, an alert button and lifeline installed on my phone, and home care for two hours three times a week. I'm now what you would call a shut in.

This could sound like life is over, but it isn't, and life is what you make it. I'm in my own home, am my own boss (or think I am). My children -- your Grandmas and Grandpas -- keep in close touch with me. My brisk walks, which I always enjoyed, are now a trip down town with my taxi driver who now after four years calls me 'Mother dear'. Wow, what a love life!

And believe it or not, you dear kids dropping in to see me and giving me a kiss and a squeeze sure brightens up my life. I eat well, sleep well and am able to read, which I enjoy so much. I also walk with a cane.

I have seen so many changes in life since I was a young girl. But I think this old world is moving much faster now than when I was young. When I watched TV showing man first walking on the moon, I knew life would never be the same – and when you folks are as old as I am, new things will be happening every day. Schools are changing, Email does away with writing letters, and progress has been made in health and in finding new medicines. You young folks know more about life than I did when I was growing up.

Trust is only a meaningless word now. But remember, even if our old world changes so that guns seem to be toys, honesty is an unknown word, children have too many activities so there is no time for Mother and Dad and togetherness, just remember that ***love never, never changes.***

Make friends, be honest, help one another, and as you become teenagers, don't think your Dad and Mother are old fuddy-duddies. They have done their best to set your feet on the right path.

Your loving Great Grandmother Belfry

The Grands and the Greats

Summertime is here again and the blue sky and puffy white clouds that Mary loved so well are dappling the earth. It is one hundred years after her birth and the world is indeed different. Her Grands and Greats are undergoing a metamorphosis too. She would be so proud to know how they are growing, changing and taking charge of their lives.

Ron and Lillian enjoyed seeing much of the world in their retirement years, taking many cruises and holidays in the UK and Europe, cavorting at the cottage with their family and feasting on Shultz donuts on Saturday mornings, a custom begun by our dad many decades ago. One especially wonderful cruise was with their whole family on a luxurious ship. What fun to be together in such a setting.

Cruising together in the Caribbean

Back row: Ron Belfry, Rob Raven, Steve Ellins, Shawn Priestman
Middle row: Lillian Belfry, Joanne Belfry Raven, Wanda Belfry Ellins, Colleen Belfry Priestman, Greg Priestman
Front row: Brooke Raven, Tyler Ellins, Breanna Ellins, Tara Raven

Ron and Lil loved seeing new places but returned often to Portugal where they had always had wonderful holidays. In January of this year they decided to visit the Algarve one more time. Their first two weeks were superb and they took time to remember some of the happiest times of their lives.

Lillian Belfry 28.11.1933 - 29.01.2007,
On the boardwalk, Praia Da Rocha, Portugal
Her last joyous day

As Lil laughingly headed for bed after beating Ron at cribbage mid-holiday she was felled by a massive stroke and suddenly their lives together were over. It was a dreadfully traumatic happening and Ron, their family and all of us were terribly shocked. She has left a huge void in all of our lives and is greatly missed. It was a very real test of Ron's courage to make final arrangements for Lil's remains before heading back to Canada alone. Lillian excelled at being a wonderful mother and grandmother to her daughters and their families and her joie de vivre and wonderful laugh will continue to live through them.

Now the next generations are spreading their wings. We'll take a minute to see where Mary and Norm's children are, what their children are doing, and how the years have treated cousins in the extended Hillis and Belfry families.

Colleen Priestman, their oldest daughter, and her partner, Sheldon Kelly, live in Unionville. Daily she commutes via Go Train to downtown Toronto to the Royal Bank. Her 25-year career there has led her to specialize in sales and sales automation.

She and Sheldon, a self employed mason with expertise in fireplace and chimney restoration, love to travel and do every chance they have.

Colleen also enjoys reading and knitting, too, much like her mothe,r Lillian, and Sheldon loves the out of doors and golfing.

Colleen Margaret Belfry Priestman

Their nest is empty during the school year as both her boys are away studying. Shawn is pursuing a business degree specialization in marketing at The University of Guelph and is in his second year. His interests include snowboarding, hockey and the environment.

Shawn and Greg Priestman

Second son, Greg, is also taking a business degree and is at Fanshawe College in London, Ontario. He has completed an electrician's course and aspires to be a self-employed electrician. Wouldn't Great-Grandfather Norm be pleased! Greg loves relaxing at the cottage, which has been a favourite place with all of Ron and Lillian's family, and he loves hockey, too.

Joanne, their second daughter, and husband, Rob Raven, live in Fonthill, Ontario, with their two daughters Tara and Brooke. Joanne has followed her Grandmother Belfry in her love and affinity for flowers and her artistic talents and their home reflects her lovely work. Joanne trained in Floristry Design, earning a diploma in Horticulture from Humber College.

Joanne Lillian Belfry Raven

For 18 years she was a floral designer/manager in Toronto, then on husband Rob's transfer she took a manager's position at a local greenhouse, where she looked after two retail greenhouses. She now works at the Royal Bank. Reading, gardening, her kids and working out at the gym are things she enjoys.

And what about her husband, Rob Raven? It has been 21 years since they met -- when she pulled him out of a snowbank one frosty winter day in Toronto. It seems she liked what she saw. They married in 1986 in a double wedding celebration with sister Wanda.

Rob has worked for the Ministry of Transportation for 27 years and his favourite hobby is buying and selling table hockey games. He loves anything to do with hockey and enjoys taking their two girls to the Buffalo Sabres games.

Their older daughter, Tara, is in her last year of High School and loves working part time at Tim Horton's. She is the social butterfly of their family and has a passion for dancing. Perhaps she will take after her Grandmother Belfry as she thinks she might get into teaching along the way.

Tara-Jo Raven

Brooke Margaret, their second daughter, entered Seventh Grade this year. Brooke follows her mother and grandmother with her artistic ability and recently melted the heart of her Granddad by designing a very special 75th birthday card for him in April. He was really touched at her thoughtful, sweet card. She has just completed Girl Guides, takes piano and hopes to grow up to be an interior decorator.

Brooke Raven

The Raven family, Joanne, Rob, Brooke and Tara

Wanda Ellins Ron and Lil's third daughter lives in Keswick with her life partner, Kevin Hewitt, and her son, Tyler, and daughter, Breanna. She is a registered real estate agent and is a manager of a large Re/Max organization in Toronto. She enjoys friends and family and the outdoors. Her partner, Kevin, is retired from 21 years in the Canadian Military and now works as a contractor when he isn't fishing or cooking.

Wanda June Belfry Ellins

Wanda's son, Tyler, loves being a Canadian Air Cadet and all the many activities involved in this endeavor through the year. Movies, video games and water tubing are some of Tyler's favourite out-of- school activities and he entered his last public school year in September.

Tyler Ambrose Ellins

His sister, Breanna, entered Grade Five this fall and loves playing with the town's rep soccer team and swimming, dancing and being with the family, especially at the cottage, which they all love. What a wise plan it was for their Belfry Grandparents to build a place for all of them to enjoy together.

Breanna Ellins

As we have heard, some of the Belfry crowd have itchy feet and our daughter and son are no exception. Quite likely my husband, Bill, and I have had something to do with their love of travelling. It has been a major part of our lives and while they were growing up in Lachine we four were on the road at every opportunity. We visited the East and West coasts, many fascinating areas of the United States, and loved one memorable month-long European adventure when the four of us sang from mountaintops, visited historical sights and revelled in castles, cottages and wee corners. The children were even enthusiastic museum hounds, having become familiar with the great Masters while helping me study for my Art History degree. What a joyous trip it was.

And too soon they were ready to continue their education in other cities and then begin adventures on their own.

When she went to Ryerson in Toronto to begin her degree in Fashion Merchandizing, our daughter, Heather, chose to use both her given names (because Heather Lynn sounded too much like a first name) thus becoming Heather-Anne. There she met her soulmate, John Hubbell, and the direction of her life changed when they married and had Raya and Jason (Jay). They moved to London, Ontario, so she could begin law studies at Western University, followed by busy years. As the mother of small children she managed her Law degree, legal positions in several places and her Masters in Tax Law, then looked for more worlds to conquer. Before they knew it they were pulling up stakes and off to live in the United Kingdom where she was offered an exciting new position. Today she is a Director at Citigroup based in London, England, and is Project Coordinator for teams in the Orient, New York and London in the field of Exotic Interest Rates.

They love life in England, as does John's mother, Rena, once a war bride, who lives with them. Their lovely home is in Farncombe, a small village southwest of London.

John Hubbell and Heather-Anne Lynn Hubbell

Travel both for work and for pleasure is a major part of their lives. John has continued his involvement with sports after his beginning experience as a skater in the Olympics. He manages a women's hockey team that has captured the British title for the last two years, plays old-timer's hockey in England, France, Slovakia, and elsewhere, has taught troubled youth and has recently earned his master's degree.

Raya Lynn Hubbell BSC, '07

Their children are becoming involved in interesting activities, too. Raya Lynn, our oldest grandchild, has this summer graduated from King's College, London University, with a BSC and is employed in a Real Estate Investment Company. She is very enthusiastic about a career in the Real Estate field and whispers to us that she intends to return to Canada to live in a few years time. How wonderful! Our fingers are crossed. Raya is an amazing downhill skier, having trained in Switzerland and New Zealand with national teams, has travelled to many countries and sparkles wherever she goes.

Grandson Jay decided several years ago that he wanted to return to Canada to complete his education so spent his last three years of high school as a boarder at Ridley College in St. Catharines. There he shone in sports with impressive successes in rugby and hockey. He loved it there and we loved having him closer to us. His visits were always a delight.

Jason Benedict Beaumont Hubbell

In June of 2006 we all gathered on Ridley's beautiful campus to see him graduate. It was a time for Raya to show parts of Canada to her special friend, Steven Walkinshaw. We were delighted to meet him and he loved Canada. Good!

Steven Walkinshaw, Raya Hubbell, Jay Hubbell, Bill Lynn, Heather-Anne Hubbell and Marg Lynn at Ridley, June 2006

The following day brother Ron and his family had a party at Joanne and Rob's home nearby and these cousins finally had a chance to meet. It was a wonderful time together.

Bill Lynn, Lillian Belfry, Marg Lynn, and Ron Belfry

Belfry brunch at Joanne's home, June 2006
Mary and Norm's grandkids, Joanne, and Rob Raven, Colleen Priestman, Heather and John Hubbell, Wanda Ellins and Kevin Hewitt

Happy Great-Grands
<u>Back row</u>: Steven Walkinshaw, Ray's friend, Raya and Jay Hubbell, Shawn and Greg Priestman
<u>Front row</u>: Brooke Raven, Breanna Ellins, Tara Raven and Tyler Ellins

But wait! The only grandson of this generation is still waiting for his place in the family saga. Our son, Brian, and his family now live in New York State and they have yet to be heard.

Brian Alexander attended Lower Canada College from Grade Five till the end of high school and his successes there became stepping-stones to Harvard, where he headed at age 17. The next four years were spent absorbing the smorgasbord of arts and sciences offered, and graduating in 1985 with a Hoopes Prize for outstanding scholarly work in his senior theses.

Brian Lynn, AB (Honour Physics), Harvard '85

He started his career in Toronto but moved to New York in the early 1990s with CIBC Wood Gundy. Janet Fryer, his wife, joined him there after a year teaching Music and Computer Science at a Scarborough High School. They loved life in the East Village of Manhattan and life was rosy with two wonderful additions to their family, first Miranda and then Benedict. A millionaire's family.

But sometimes world happenings cause folks to change directions....

That happened to this Lynn family after the trauma of 9/11. Brian's too close proximity to the situation was unsettling. Some deep soul-searching convinced them that Brian should follow his heart and begin his own business, a long-time dream.

Soon their condo was rented and they left the corporate world for a wooded country home in the Catskills, where their waterfall garden is relaxing, their very own pond is more fun than concrete, and the deer flit through the pines. Who needs Manhattan?

Miranda Elisabeth had been drawing, sculpting and painting with various art mediums since she was a very little girl and exhibits a creative mind and amazing artistic skill. At eleven she reads voraciously, loves drama and acting in the Shakespearian productions for which her Mom Janet designs and creates the costumes and writes and produces the music.

Miranda Elisabeth Lynn

Miranda and her eight-year-old brother Benedict Thomas love performing in these productions and also enjoy being part of Janet's children's orchestra in which Miranda plays the flute and Ben punctuates the action on the trumpet. And sometimes when they visit, they all serenade us with their flutes and recorders for our pleasure.

Benedict, Janet and Miranda, 'The Taming of the Shrew' Woodstock, N.Y., Summer 2006

Miranda, Janet, Brian and Ben accept flowers after a concert in Kingston, New York, spring 2007

Benedict is in grade three and loves trains, anything that goes, and his Grandfather Bill, who helps him build things and takes him to the train museum when he comes for a visit. He also likes the fact that his name 'Benedict' is Granddad Bill's middle name and his paternal Great-Grandma's family name. He will likely follow his dad and grandfathers in the sciences.

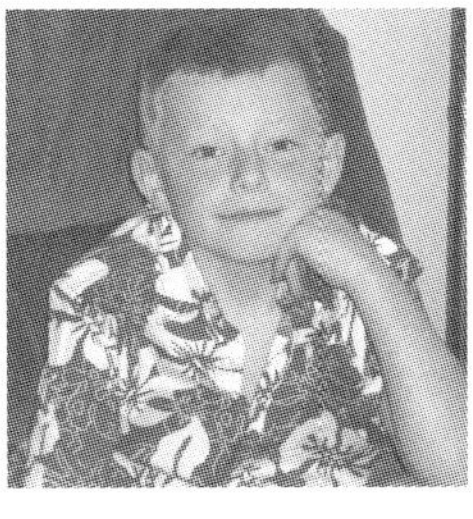

Benedict Thomas Lynn

Brian's business continues to flourish as he creates software for the corporate world and consults for ISDA, giving seminars for the international market. In his spare time he is writing scientific material about processes he has developed.

Before Jay's graduation all of our family had orders to circle their calendars so we could be sure to have everyone here for a special time together. No easy feat! And happen it did the week after Jay's grad. It was great to see the younger children cavort with their older cousins and all the big ones catch up with each other.

John and Heather-Anne Hubbell and Janet and Brian Lynn

Benedict and Miranda Lynn and Raya and Jay Hubbell

Games, kite flying, presents, and laughter were high on the agenda for that special time. We do wish those miles between our homes would evaporate once in a while.

The rest of the Grands and Greats

<u>Back row</u>: Bill Lynn, John and Heather-Anne Hubbell, Marg Lynn, Jay and Raya Hubbell, Janet Fryer Lynn and Brian Lynn

<u>Front row</u>: Miranda and Benedict Lynn

We think Mary and Norm would have enjoyed getting to know their enlarged family as we have loved meeting the colourful characters that have gone before us. What an interesting mix of skills and creative approaches to life there have been. These Grands and Greats will surely continue to add spice to our family and to the grand tapestry of life. As parents, grandparents, uncles, aunts and cousins we will cheer them on.

During this search for details of our relatives, we've connected with cousins who remember the glory days when we were young and our parents made getting together a priority. It has been a special experience.

The Hillis family has lost first cousin Jack Hudson, but I have had valuable photos and information about the family from his brother Jim and wife, Isabel, who were such a thoughtful niece and nephew to Mary and Norm and Aunt Jean. Aunt Bea's Harrison family has suffered the loss of cousins Earl, Jean and Ross but their children are thriving and continuing the work their parents began. Cousin Jean, was always ready to visit Mary and she cared and shared ancestor information before her death in 2006.

Jim and Isabel Hillis
and two daughters, Carole and Marion
with Mary

Our Belfry Cousins

And what are our Belfry cousins doing these days? The Bala Belfrys have lost cousin Don who died of heart complications after several years of illness although he and Bobbie were able to take several trips to see their daughter Jane and family in Australia.

Cousin Gloria is ready anytime to supply answers to questions and to offer her support, and is indeed the matriarch of the clan. However, her world has just been rocked by the recent death of her beloved husband, Bob Arkinson. Emphysema and severe heart problems caused his death in late August of this year. And so we cousins met again to remember him and also to reconnect with each other and share the happenings in our lives. Gloria and sis Marjorie have enjoyed some recent visits to see Marj's daughters some of whom we had the pleasure of meeting, along with Marnie Dixon and Taylor, Gloria and Bob's children, and their extended families.

Marjorie Belfry Madden, Ron Belfry and Gloria Belfry Arkinson, September 2007

Herb Rodell, June's husband was also there, and with eyes flashing, he recounted the first time he saw June on 40th Avenue in New York and how he pestered her until she finally went out with him several months later. He had decided that she would be his bride, and so she was!

Marjorie and I had time to visit and remembered sleeping at our Grandma Belfry's when she, June and I shared a bed giggling half the night. We laughed again at the candlelight church service we all attended in Uxbridge in our youth when we cousins sat in the pew behind our aunts. In her usual flamboyant style, Aunt Lu was wearing a spectacular hat with a feathered bird on top. And she was sitting under one of the bank of candles placed strategically around the church. During the service someone glanced up and noticed white candle drippings slowly forming on Aunt Lu's coat, right under the feathered bird. Nudges were quickly passed and our whole pew shook with our laughter. I'm sure our mothers were not thrilled with our performance that night but I chuckle every time I think of it. What memories....

Marg and Ron, September, 2007

Because our respective homes are about ten hours apart by car, Ron and I appreciate these occasions for brother/sister times together, too, and they are very important to both of us. We have managed several visits and many emails and phone calls in this last year, and find they make those people we love feel closer.

Cousin Larry Belfry and his lovely wife, Betty, had lived through his repeated bouts of cancer since 1999 but, sadly, he lost his battle in May of this year in his 60th year. Despite the illnesses and painful medical treatments, he and Betty were very happy and took many holidays and cruises together. Their families and friends gave them much joy and now those memories, too, are very special.

My phone often brings cheery greetings from Cousin Lee and we love remembering funny happenings of our youth. I have really appreciated her thorough genealogical research and incorporated many aspects of it in the Belfry/Ney resume. It is interesting how discussing a long-forgotten memory can bring such a rush of pleasure. She and Ken are celebrating their 50th Anniversary this year with a European River Cruise and party, bringing to mind the celebration we shared so long ago for our Belfry Grandparents.

Doris Belfry Burke and Lee Belfry Bryen

Oct. 2007: Ken and Lee Bryen celebrate 50 years

I appreciated speaking with my cousin Nelda and her husband some months ago but only very recently have connected with her brother Gar (Garnet) who is the father of three boys, grandfather of six and still playing hockey and teaching golf in Ontario where he and Peggy live. What a tribe!

Bill and I are finding retirement very much to our liking. He retired from Foxboro as a Senior Automatic Control specialist after 35 years of service designing control theory for many large industries. It was especially interesting for him to be asked do some consulting work in Queensland, Australia, thus allowing me the opportunity to join him there three times. It is a marvellous continent and we loved exploring all of its states and capital cities, as well as many fascinating beauty spots.

RMC 50th Graduation of Class of '57
September 2007

I 'graduated' from Selwyn House School in Westmount after 16 satisfying years as a classroom teacher and Department Head of Elementary English. It was a stimulating environment where teachers had many opportunities to share in decision making and programme development. It is always a thrill to see 'my boys' now as young men making their mark in the world.

We are involved in Summerlea United Church and community activities such as shopping for Meals on Wheels, genealogy research, concerts, reading, spending too much time on our computers, and continuing to visit our families and travel the world.

In quiet times I sit in my rocking chair and remember those many stories that have been such a part of the lives of our families. I am awed by the host of amazing players whose lives have shaped ours in ways they could never have imagined. Could we have had the courage to leave all of our loved ones and cross the ocean for such an uncertain future? I'm not quite sure.

What a debt of gratitude we owe to those ancestors and adventurers who did take the challenges. They ultimately forged new settlements, building homes and lives in what was a young, untried country.

And by their actions they have handed us an amazing legacy!

Life has been very good to our generation. In order that the vision and contribution of our many forefathers will not be forgotten, we must remember to be enthusiastic storytellers and recorders. The children of our generation will have the wings to soar wherever they wish if we share the love and encouragement we have received. And above all, if we really become serious about trying to keep our country free and safe, our loved ones will enjoy a beautiful, healthy environment in which to grow and thrive.

About the Author

Teaching, reading, writing, and social histories have held a fascination for Margaret Belfry Lynn during her lifetime. She has taught in East York, Ontario, in France on loan to the DND Schools, and in Montreal, where, before retirement, she was Head of Elementary English at Selwyn House School in Westmount. Her academic credentials include a joint major in Education and Art History and diplomas in Teaching, Special Education and Art. She and her husband, Bill Lynn -- parents of two grown children and grandparents of four -- have enjoyed the fascinating searches that this journey to find her forefathers has created for them.

Family Notes

Family Notes

Family Notes

Family Notes

Family Notes

Family Notes

Family Notes

Family Notes

Family Notes

Family Notes

Family Notes